# RURAL ESCAPES

# RURAL ESCAPES

## A CELEBRATION OF NORTH AMERICAN COUNTRY HOMES

RYLAND
PETERS
& SMALL

London  New York

First published in the USA in 2002
This paperback edition published in 2009 by
Ryland Peters & Small, Inc.
519 Broadway, 5th Floor
New York, NY 10012

Ryland Peters & Small
20–21 Jockey's Fields
London WC1R 4BW

10 9 8 7 6 5 4 3 2 1

ISBN 978-1-84597-890-7

The hardcover edition of this book was cataloged
as follows:

Library of Congress Cataloging-in-Publication Data

Rural escapes : a celebration of North American
homes / by Jo Denbury ... [et al.].
    p. cm.
    Includes index.
    ISBN: 1-84172-327-4
    1. Country homes--Decoration--United
States. 2. Interior decoration--United States-
-History--20th century. I. Denbury, Jo.

NK2195 .R87 R87 2002
747`.0973--dc21
                                        2002024946

SENIOR EDITOR  Clare Double
LOCATION AND PICTURE RESEARCH MANAGER
Kate Brunt
PICTURE RESEARCHER  Emily Westlake
PRODUCTION  Patricia Harrington

ART DIRECTOR  Gabriella Le Grazie
PUBLISHING DIRECTOR  Alison Starling

www.rylandpeters.com

Printed in China

# CONTENTS

# INTRODUCTION

*by Bo Niles*

America, in a way, has always been about escape. As the "land of opportunity" and "land of promise," America is where people from virtually every nation on earth could—and can—make a new start, create a new life, and find a new home. Once these goals have been achieved, escape evolves to mean any number of things. For some, it involves physical activity. For others, it requires intellectual pursuit. For still others, escape is a spiritual quest. Often, and happily, the three combine in a place apart: a rural escape. As a retreat from the everyday, a rural escape—be it a primary residence or a home away from home—reinvigorates the body, reactivates the mind, and refreshes the soul. It is oasis.

Nothing connotes a sense of repose as much as water, especially when the sky appears to rest upon its limpid surface. Water reflects the whims of weather as well as the ebb and flow of our most deeply felt emotions.

OPPOSITE:
On Long Island, New York, a quiet inlet is fed by the salt waters of the Atlantic Ocean.

RIGHT:
Granite boulders high-step into a tranquil lake in Maine.

Although escape inspired many of the immigrants who made their way across the oceans to America, it was not the primary goal of the valiant navigators and explorers who first set foot upon the continent. For them, the vast landmass that rose up out of the Atlantic shocked their expectations. This wilderness, after all, was not the expected target of their westward venture into unknown waters. Asia was. What explorers such as Christopher Columbus, Alvar Nunez, Hernando de Soto, and others sought was an easy, waterborne alternative to the daunting overland passage to the Orient and the unfathomable riches they coveted, spice and gold. Instead, they discovered a different treasure: a New World.

Just six years after Columbus's historic voyage, in 1498, Englishman John Cabot sailed the entire Atlantic coastline of the nation that would eventually be called America. Very soon after his explorations, escape, rather than riches, became the prime rationale for the arduous westward journey to this wilderness: Escape from bigotry and religious persecution; escape from famine; escape from terror; escape from dire poverty, or overcrowding, or loss of land—or all of the above.

In the earliest years of exploration and settlement, these intrepid souls merely replaced one set of dangers with another. Thousands died from disease and exposure to brutal winters and humid, mosquito-ridden summers. As the years passed, though, and each succeeding group of settlers grew more sophisticated about adapting to their surroundings, escape to this New World began to be guided by the rich potential for a life marked by individual choice and by independence. America was hailed as a land of opportunity, a place where, for better or worse, those who made the effort to immigrate would be free to live as they chose. Within twenty years of the Pilgrims' landing at Plymouth, Massachusetts, almost a quarter of a million souls had settled in New England. Within seven generations, the citizens of this New World felt themselves to be distinctly, and distinctively, "American." They declared themselves a nation. The Thirteen Colonies became the United States of America.

In many instances, a rural retreat is just that: an isolated sanctuary that, by choice, is at a considerable remove from civilization.

FAR LEFT:
In a family camp in the Adirondack Mountains of New York State, privacy is assured because access is by boat across a lake. Daily life revolves around outdoor recreation—or indoor activities around the fire.

LEFT:
In the mountains, nights turn cool, even in high summer, necessitating an ample supply of cordwood.

BELOW:
A Colonial house in Maine holds the domestic pleasures of its interior in reserve.

OPPOSITE:
A field in Pennsylvania slowly succumbs to the influence of Mother Nature; in due course it will revert to forest.

## THE ALLURE OF ESCAPE ECHOES THE DESIRE FOR FREEDOM THAT PROPELLED THE ORIGINAL PIONEERS ON THEIR HISTORIC MIGRATIONS TO AND ACROSS THE AMERICAN CONTINENT.

Still, the concept of escape persisted. As each new wave of immigrants abandoned a life in an Old World they knew well for one they could barely imagine, another, older generation of colonists was exchanging their already familiar American way of life for another in unknown territory. Pioneers, including frontiersmen such as Daniel Boone, pressed ever southward and westward, taming the wilderness and transforming it into homestead, farmstead, plantation, town, and, eventually, city. By the early 1900s, escaping to and settling in America had assumed the mantle of myth; more and more people continued to arrive, thousands upon thousands of them. Between 1892 and 1924, over twelve million immigrants passed through Ellis Island in New York harbor. Today, they still arrive, with hope, from every corner of the globe, some legally, some without passport. America now officially numbers some 290 million persons, representing virtually every nationality on earth.

In a very real sense, the allure of escape, and especially rural escape—be it for a weekend, or a vacation, or even for an afternoon—echoes the desire for freedom that propelled the original pioneers on their historic migrations to and across the American continent.

As a form of leisure, though, it did not evolve until the onset of the so-called Gilded Age, which coincided with the Industrial Revolution. Until then, most people worked too hard to take time off; most did not have the discretionary income to travel far from home. But, with the advent of the railroad and the invention of the automobile, wealthy financiers and entrepreneurs redefined the concept of escape—as the impetus for leisure. Many of the new rich traveled and collected art. Many, following the example of sportsman and President Theodore Roosevelt—who added millions of acres to the National Park system—were drawn to the recreational opportunities afforded by the outdoors, believing fervently that the wilderness could be mastered as a domain for recreation and entertainment. Instead of escaping from the wilderness, they escaped into it.

During the Gilded Age, too, America experienced her Centennial, which ignited a resurgence of interest in the architecture and mores of the past. A Colonial Revival

was spearheaded by some of the very same financiers and collectors of the era, who went on to construct museums extolling the designs and values of the Founding Fathers: Henry Ford, for example, built Greenfield Village, near Detroit, Michigan; Henry Francis du Pont erected his immense Winterthur outside Wilmington, Delaware, and the Rockefellers restored Williamsburg, Virginia. Photographer Wallace Nutting created and sold millions of color-enhanced photographic images of nostalgic evocations of Colonial life, especially interiors of Early American country homes.

When constructing their most rustic getaways, the wealthy took as their inspiration the same kind of unpretentious dwelling places Wallace Nutting esteemed. Early American home styles were revived and glorified to

oftentimes outrageous proportions in vacation retreats in out-of-the-way venues, such as the Adirondack Mountains of New York State and the rugged coastline of Maine: the humble log cabin, for example, evolved into the Great Camp or lodge, and the demure Cape was transformed into the shingled "cottage"—both built on a grand scale and boasting literally dozens of rooms. The so-called Robber Barons' version of the simple life echoed French Queen Marie Antoinette's retreat to her "little farm": escape as play, supported by armies of servants and every comfort imaginable.

After a Depression and two World Wars, America entered a cycle of peace and prosperity that was followed, during the 1960s and 1970s, by a period of internal crisis and upheaval. The Civil Rights movement, the assassinations of John F. and Robert Kennedy and Martin Luther King, Jr., and the Vietnam War caused

many Americans living in the burgeoning suburbs and cities to turn to nature for solace. A number became hippies and "dropped out" into remote rural areas; others decided to spend their precious leisure time at one remove from the towns and urban areas where they worked and made their home. Rural escape promised a liberating sense of sanctuary.

In 1976, America also celebrated her second centennial—the Bicentennial—and once again focused her interest on the nation's unique design heritage. Sparked by books and magazines extolling Early American and American Country styles, millions searched out old houses they could restore, and furnishings and accessories that wore a patina of age. New construction of the period mimicked Colonial prototypes, as well as mid-nineteenth-century farmhouses and log cabins; reproduction furniture was

Everyone has his or her own vision of escape.

ABOVE LEFT:
For some, retreat affords an opportunity to rescue, reclaim, and preserve a precious piece of America's architectural heritage; an example is this brick factory in New Jersey that was converted into a cozy home-away-from-home.

ABOVE:
The opportunity for escape may also present itself as a mandate to create something utterly new. In Maine, an artist's retreat in the woods is both a haven and a work of art.

**AS THE NEW MILLENNIUM TAKES SHAPE, AND THE WORLD BECOMES MORE AND MORE UNCERTAIN OF ITS FUTURE, AMERICANS ARE MORE EAGER THAN EVER BEFORE TO ESCAPE THE CONTINUOUS ASSAULT OF INFORMATION AND HYPE.**

mass-produced, with editions of line-for-line copies of their antecedents. In the 1980s and 1990s, the ever-popular Country style began to be infused more and more with regional and ethnic overtones, which added richness, depth, and texture to the American Country home.

Today, the desire—especially for rural escape—retains a primal urgency to get back in touch with nature as well as back to basics, but, in our computer-dominated Information Age, it also derives from a wish to withdraw, at least for awhile, from lives on overload. As the new millennium takes shape, and the world becomes more and more uncertain of its future, Americans are more eager than ever before to escape the continuous assault of information and hype imposed by the news and the media. Some continue to seek refuge in homes that focus on outdoor recreational activities such as sailing, hiking, fishing, or skiing, while others ask little of their retreat, other than that it be comfortable enough so that, when they kick off their shoes, they can relax and absorb the beauty of their surroundings, without effort or hassle. Some travel a great distance to revive their spirits in settings that differ dramatically from where they live most of the year. Others grab the chance to create an environment that conjures up memories of beloved grandparents' lives and homes.

# A RURAL ESCAPE IS WHERE WE CAN BE SPONTANEOUS AND ADVENTUROUS, RELAXED AND FULL OF ENERGY. IT IS WHERE WE FEEL MOST FREE. AND THAT, AT ROOT, IS WHAT ESCAPE TO AND WITHIN AMERICA IS ABOUT.

The twenty-four houses contained within the four chapters of this book bear witness to the all-American ideal of the self-reliant individual, as well as reverence for the land. Colonial retreats take their cue from the first, primitive shingle- and clapboard-sheathed abodes erected by earliest settlers in New England. Two purist variations on the Colonial theme are the Shaker and the Quaker, both outgrowths of religious traditions based on a quest for simplicity and perfection as expressive of a devotion to God. Shaker- and Quaker-inspired interiors exhibit balance, order, and symmetry; these homes are practical, harmonious, and serene.

Rustic homesteads are typically built to preserve as much of the surrounding landscape as possible. Resourceful, pragmatic, and utilitarian, they pose an aesthetic that goes hand in hand with eco-friendly adaptation to nature, and they utilize recycled lumber and logs to celebrate their affinity for their surroundings. Even when sited on a small lot, rustic houses tend to be embraced by "green belt," land decreed to be forever wild. Proponents of the Arts & Crafts Movement, like the Shakers, underscore the belief that the home and its furnishings "have a profound moral influence upon the individual and society"; thus, rustic retreats in the Craftsman tradition are honest and straightforward, too.

ABOVE LEFT AND RIGHT: Direct contact with nature is one of the chief pleasures of getting away from it all, especially from the city. But that dialogue need not mean that a weekend or vacation home be devoid of an urbane sophistication or sensibility. In fact, gutsy materials typically affiliated with the urban environment—concrete, steel, and glass—can be transformed into an aerie that feels as at home in the forest as on a boulevard in town. In this modern interpretation of a treehouse, ample expanses of glass appear to pull the forest, and its play on shadow and light, right into the house.

Pioneers of the New Frontier Spirit live out the legacy of author–philosopher Henry David Thoreau, who retired to a cabin built with his own hands on the pond that bears the name of his most famous volume: Walden. Like him, proto-homesteaders infected with the New Frontier Spirit go to great lengths to realize their notion of escape in as simple and carefree a manner as they can—be it in a ride-and-park Airstream, a jungle garden near the Pacific Ocean, or a beach commune on the shore of Long Island, New York. Some require no specific grounding at all; for them, escape is simplicity itself: a hammock, a treehouse, a shack, or a tent, where they feel well away from the cares of the world.

Homes that manifest Contemporary Inspirations are pared to their essentials yet retain an air of urbanity even in the most remote settings. Whether converted from an existing structure, like a former brick factory in New Jersey, or constructed anew, they employ materials and design devices, such as large expanses of glass, decks, and patios to bring the outdoors in.

As you can see from the variety of houses featured in the book, escape is an intensely personal experience. More than that, though, the feeling at the base of every retreat is instinctual and primal: a need to feel secure and comfortable. A primary residence may offer both, but a rural escape often provides more. A rural escape is where we can be spontaneous and adventurous, relaxed and full of energy. It is, in sum, where we feel most free. And that, at root, is what escape to and within America is all about.

# COLONIAL
## CHARM

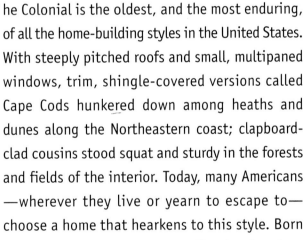

T he Colonial is the oldest, and the most enduring, of all the home-building styles in the United States. With steeply pitched roofs and small, multipaned windows, trim, shingle-covered versions called Cape Cods hunkered down among heaths and dunes along the Northeastern coast; clapboard-clad cousins stood squat and sturdy in the forests and fields of the interior. Today, many Americans —wherever they live or yearn to escape to— choose a home that hearkens to this style. Born of necessity as crude, yet effective bastions against weather and wilderness, Colonial homesteads evolved over time into practical, sober, and dignified houses that incorporate many values Americans hold dear. Colonial homes are warm and welcoming. They offer cozy

respite from the vagaries of the world. And, they are easy to care for. Their intimate dialogue with wood also serves as a vivid souvenir of America's collective history. Wood, like culture, acquires a patina as time goes by. Exposed rafters and framing timbers, beamed ceilings, paneled walls, and wide-board floors provide a hospitable background for comfortable, pared-down furnishings and homespun textiles, as well as for collections that reflect personal passion and taste. The Colonial home is remarkably resilient and responsive to virtually any lifestyle. That is why it is so popular and easy to love.

LEFT:
After the fire, the owner was allowed to rebuild on the same "footprint" as the old house, and decided that everything should look as though it had been there forever. The architects were commissioned to replace the cottage not with a replica, but with a year-round home providing the equivalent amount of peace, quiet, and memories.

RIGHT:
Porches surround the house. Shingles cover the outside veranda walls, with chairs and other woodwork painted Shaker blue, while rocking chairs stand on plain bleached-wood floors. The dog, like everyone who comes here, loves the lake.

# LUCKY STRIKE

This photographer's remote lakeside cottage in Maine, bought as a summer weekend retreat, burned down in 1992. The cottage's replacement is such a success that it is now her main home, year round. With wild and wonderful weather—ice so thick it freezes the lake in winter—plus birds, moose, beavers, otters, and wilderness, this charming rebuilt home is a total contrast to her second home in San Francisco. To its owner, it has provided a new way of living.

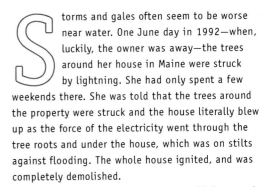

ABOVE:
**The new waterside "cottage" has now become the owner's main home, while her second home is in California, where her mother and sister live. And, yes, commuting between the wilderness and San Francisco does amount to culture shock.**

LEFT AND ABOVE RIGHT:
**Here, as in most of the house, colors are subordinated to the views: the chairs are upholstered in neutrals. Everywhere there are comfortable chairs cushioned in well-washed fabrics.**

Storms and gales often seem to be worse near water. One June day in 1992—when, luckily, the owner was away—the trees around her house in Maine were struck by lightning. She had only spent a few weekends there. She was told that the trees around the property were struck and the house literally blew up as the force of the electricity went through the tree roots and under the house, which was on stilts against flooding. The whole house ignited, and was completely demolished.

The owner admits that, now, she's glad it happened. "The fact that it burned down changed a lot for me. Without that, I might not have moved here. It was actually worse, in a way, to lose the trees."

The fire presented the chance to start again and rebuild on the same site, a mere six feet from the water's edge. If it had not occurred, she would not have been allowed to change the tiny cottage, but the state authorities agreed that she could create another house on the same "footprint."

The owner has lived by the lake since 1995 and says it is fabulous. One reason is the constant changes wrought by the water. "The lake freezes in winter and the ice is usually covered in snow—so we do a lot of skiing and other activities on the water. My dog just loves to run around on the ice. Then ice fishermen come and put up shacks all around us. It's not very picturesque, but we have a lot of laughs watching what they get up to—drinking beer and slapping each other on the back."

There are bass, perch, landlocked salmon, and trout in the lake, and colorful water birds. "The loons are the principal birds here. They're large and

not too good on land, so they mostly need to paddle. They nest by the shore, but we do our best to leave them alone. They are magnificent to look at—black with white accent feathers."

Other wildfowl make the lake a migratory stop. Bufflehead ducks and hooded mergansers come in their hundreds and may stay for only a day. Chickadees—the state bird of Maine—visit, as well as bluebirds and redwing blackbirds. Native blueberry and huckleberry bushes provide berries for the birds to eat. There are deer in the area, and moose have been sighted here—the owner has seen footprints in her front yard. An otter lives on the property. There are wild turkeys, and beavers came one year.

The beavers proceeded to cut down one of the poplars—apparently their favorite—but so far the wonderful hemlocks, cedar evergreens, and pines, along with the oaks, maples, beeches, and birches that cluster on the point, have survived intact.

THE LAKE FREEZES IN WINTER AND THE ICE IS USUALLY COVERED IN SNOW—SO WE DO A LOT OF SKIING AND OTHER ACTIVITIES ON THE WATER. MY DOG LOVES TO RUN AROUND ON THE ICE. THEN ICE FISHERMEN COME AND PUT UP SHACKS AROUND US.

As the living room windows overlook the waters of the lake, who could resist placing a carved wooden swan where he can admire the view? Lake-washed pebbles make a pleasing display high up on the stone central chimney.

LEFT AND ABOVE:
The tiny guest room has a fine log-cabin quilt on the bed. Under the gables, the windows are small and simple, and the architectural detailing is straightforward and rugged.

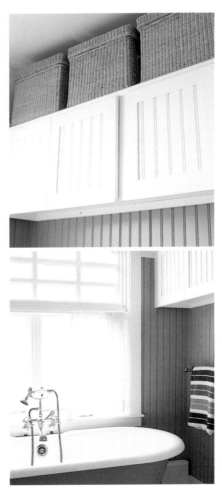

LEFT AND ABOVE:
The bed in the owner's room is covered in a favorite quilt from her mother and a newer one from Ralph Lauren. Her bedroom suite has water views in three directions, with morning light to the bathtub, southerly views down the lake, and sunset in a small reading nook.

RIGHT:
Natural wickerwork storage baskets are ranged above white wood-planked cabinets in the bathroom, while translucent white curtains shade its windows. The blue paint on walls and tub recalls the porch.

The weather is the opposite of California's. "It can be very windy and stormy but also quite lovely, magnificent. One phenomenon that happens in April is that the ice breaks up in the lake and flows with the current to one end. A couple of years ago, the wind changed as this was happening and started pushing the ice up to my house. The ice piled up all around the shore, and I was afraid it was going to come up onto the porch. It was extraordinary—in little pieces like ice cubes, piling up toward me and tinkling as they rolled over...bizarre and scary."

When the ice is intact, however, the owner can skate along the lake as far as the little local town, while in summer the town can be reached in her own small sailing boat. She has also taken a fishing boat with a motor to town and paddled a canoe there, as well as sailing friends to a local restaurant in summer. Also in summer, she can entertain friends at home, eating out on the open porch (well screened against the mosquitoes).

The house is also a work space—the owner is a photographer creating fine-art prints. And she takes pictures of her particular stretch of lake, which is 11 miles long in total, in all its moods.

Since the terrible day of the lightning strike the trees and underbrush have regrown, and the house is settling down to look even more mature and established. Perhaps it was a lucky strike after all.

OPPOSITE TOP:
The farmhouse turns
its face to the sun, its
bright, white painted
porch beaming in
welcome to all who
enter by the gate in
the split-rail fence.

OPPOSITE BELOW LEFT:
A pair of whimsical
hoop-back chairs made
from horseshoes flanks
the front door and a
dry sink brimming over
with impatience. Blue-
and-white floor stripes
are the same width as
the porch posts.

OPPOSITE BELOW RIGHT:
Anyone have a key to
the mailbox?

ABOVE:
The new fieldstone
patio was built around
a stand of birches.

In much of the Northeast, the earth breeds rocks. During the Colonial era, they were a farmer's bane. As he pulled them from the soil, more pressed to the surface. Sisyphean in his labors, the farmer shouldered the stones and transformed them into walls to surround his fields or shelter his family, and, in many cases, prized livestock as well. The bucolic hills of eastern Pennsylvania host many stone houses. Many, like this one, are weekend retreats from New York or Philadelphia.

# HILLSIDE FARMHOUSE

## DARK, STAINED BEAMS CRISSCROSS THE CEILINGS; EXPOSING THE BEAMS LENDS AN ILLUSION OF HEIGHT AND REMOVES ANY FEELINGS OF BEING CRAMPED.

**LEFT:**
A quartet of delicate, comb-back Windsor chairs encircles a table in front of the living-room fireplace. The tuxedo-style sofa is upholstered in a red-and-white checked cotton that recalls dishtoweling used at many a country kitchen sink. The seat cushion stretches the entire length of the sofa, so it can double as a place for a snooze.

**ABOVE:**
Toweling threaded along tension rods covers the lowest panes of each window.

Like many houses and barns in this county, the stone farmhouse straddles a slope. Barns were purposely designed on two or three levels: the lowest housed a farmer's herd of milking cows, the one immediately above, his team of horses, and, perhaps, a carriage, while the top—or hayloft— stored the hay that would be pitched down to the feeding troughs. A house constructed in such a manner dropped at the back so that the kitchen, on the lowest level, could be insulated by a berm of earth and rock, and thus retain heat radiated by the cookstove during the winter. The berm also allowed the room to stay cool when the weather warmed. The owner of this weekend house need not worry about such matters, though; electric baseboard heating could be—and was— retrofitted into the existing structure without compromising the integrity of the house. Fireplaces abound, too; one warms virtually every room.

Utilities aside, the house responded beautifully to renovation. On the exterior, the stonework required some repointing where mortar in the joints had eroded. Nine-over-six windows were restored, and new, combination screen–storm windows installed as further protection against heat loss— and to keep out insects when the windows are raised.

RIGHT:
Unlike most
checkerboard floors,
which are painted
on the bias, the one
in the kitchen runs
parallel to the walls.
These checks are
smaller than the norm,
which adds to their
sense of liveliness.
A folding wooden
screen pulls across the
walk-in fireplace to
shut out drafts.

BELOW:
A trousseau-worthy
damask tablecloth
wears a monogram: R.

With its standing-seam tin roof and straightforward columns—and no railing—the front porch, which probably was appended to the house sometime after it was built, presents a cheerful face to host and guests alike. Rather than leave the back wall stone, the owner faced it with stucco and painted it white, along with the shutters and the front door. The floor is also painted, but in jazzy blue and white striations, in a whimsical salute to the Stars and Stripes.

Part of the charm of the house derives from the cozy proportions of the rooms. Because of the thickness of the stone walls, window recesses are deep, offering sills that can double as windowseats. Dark, stained beams crisscross the ceilings; exposing the beams, rather than covering them with wallboard and plastering them as many homeowners are wont to do, lends an illusion of height and removes any feelings of being cramped. Most of the floors are stained, too, except for the one in the kitchen, which is painted with sprightly checks in the same blue and white as the porch stripes.

Although sparsely furnished, the interiors are eminently welcoming. An all-American palette prevails here, adding red to the mix in the living room through the use of upholstery and window skirts based on utilitarian dishtoweling. In this haven of calm, hospitality reigns.

ABOVE AND LEFT:
A collection of blue-and-white spongeware—and other favorite blue pieces, including a number of tankards and two graduated sets of canisters—fills a massive, open slant-front cupboard in the kitchen. To make it easier to entertain a crowd, stacks of dishes are gathered on the lower shelves.

OPPOSITE TOP LEFT
AND ABOVE:
Split-rail fences
meander along the
graveled drive, and
across the lawn,
separating both from
the field beyond.

MAIN PICTURE:
The front door opens
directly, without
apology, into a large,
open living area that
is dominated by a
whitewashed cupboard.

OPPOSITE CENTER:
The finest, widest
planks of wood were
usually reserved to
panel the fireplace
wall in the main room
of a house. Here, the
elegant, eighteenth-
century-inspired wing
chair and settee are
slipcased in white
homespun. A
collection of early
pewter stretches along
the overmantel.

OPPOSITE BOTTOM:
Every fireplace wears
a mantel in a
different style.

RIGHT:
The owner tucked a
built-in guest bed
under the eaves.

Nestled in the woods on the outskirts of Litchfield, Connecticut, this restored clapboard-covered house takes a place in American history. Built by Oliver Wolcott, later one of the signatories to the Declaration of Independence, the eighteenth-century house now sits on a 14-acre wooded site. When the town of Litchfield was laid out in 1717, its planners deemed this size appropriate to a "townhouse building plot." The house's front door is original, with the original hardware. The portico was added around 1790, and its gilded fanlight is said to represent the "rising sun" of the American nation. The yard is an interpretation of its nineteenth-century predecessor. "Skeletal" elements of the older yard have been found. In the orchard behind the house, while the American War of Independence was raging, the women and children of Litchfield melted down a statue of King George III for bullets to use against the British soldiers.

This vacation home is not just a place to escape to. It has become a place of pilgrimage for the couple who lovingly, and meticulously, restored it. To visit this majestic Colonial home, built by a man who devoted his life to democracy, is to visit a glorious and gracious epoch of America's history. HISTORIC LANDMARK

# THE OWNERS' RECREATION OF THE MOST GLORIOUS PERIOD OF AMERICAN HISTORY HAS GIVEN THEM AN ESCAPE FROM THE TECHNOLOGY-OBSESSED TWENTIETH CENTURY TO A MORE GRACIOUS, LEISURELY AGE, WHEN ORDINARY MEN COULD STILL ACCOMPLISH GREAT THINGS.

The house was built in 1754 for Oliver Wolcott, Sr., then Colonial High Sheriff of Litchfield, Connecticut. Wolcott later became one of the signatories to the Declaration of Independence, and in 1780, and again in 1781, he played host to George Washington in this Litchfield home. The ideals to which Wolcott had devoted his life were enshrined in the Declaration he signed, and he died, a happy man, in the house he built, in 1797.

With the passing of the years, the house, with its typical Colonial "center chimney" hall and massive chimney stack, fell into disrepair. It was in a sorry state when it came into the hands of its present owners, the chairman of a private investment firm in New York and his interior-designer wife.

For them, it was the vacation home they were looking for, but it was not just a house, but a place

RIGHT:
**The library is furnished with an assortment of country furniture, while the oil painting, *Niagara Falls*, is an American work dated around 1840–60.**

ABOVE RIGHT AND OPPOSITE:
**Many features of the house remain unaltered. Original, hand-routed, beaded clapboards protect the house's exterior; even the wide floorboards of the second floor are still held in place with the original handmade nails.**

of pilgrimage, and as such it deserved to be restored with respect. Their labor of love has resulted in an edifice that is not only a shrine to democracy, but also a comfortable and beautiful New England home.

The house retains the character and atmosphere of a classic Colonial home. This is thanks to the present owners, for whom it was essential that the restoration be carried out accurately and sympathetically. To help them in their endeavor, they enlisted an expert from the Society for the Preservation of New England Architecture, who carried out a paint analysis, thus ensuring that the paint colors used were authentic. In addition, they employed a firm of woodwork and plaster restorers who adhered strictly to eighteenth-century techniques. The result is a home that is simple and cozy but stylish, just as would have befitted the high-minded gentleman and soldier who built it.

The highlight of Wolcott's house must surely be the Keeping, or Long Room, pictured on this page. This room, with its cooking fire and its original twelve-over-twelve windows, would have been at the heart of Wolcott's home. Now it houses a number of his letters and some early etchings. The room has a fine seventeenth-century English oak gateleg table and an eighteenth-century fishing-rod rack to complement the oil paintings of fish displayed nearby. Also of interest is a nineteenth-century candle chandelier made of wrought iron, hanging over the gateleg table.

ABOVE:
The paneling in the dining room is original. The windows were "modernized" in about 1888 with the addition of larger panes of glass.

LEFT AND FAR LEFT:
The Keeping Room retains its original wide oak floorboards and virgin "old growth" wide-plank pine paneling below the chair rail, but the paneling above the fireplace is a reconstruction. The American Colonies were not allowed a glass industry, so the windowpanes in the room are made from the largest size of glass that could be imported from England. It was a size that stowed easily in a ship's hold.

RIGHT:
This corner cabinet was added to the dining room in about 1790 as part of the decorations carried out by Wolcott to celebrate America's independence. The wainscoting dates from 1754, when the house was built.

LEFT:
The fine staircase, dating from about 1770, when "center hall" architecture came to Litchfield, leads to the five bedrooms on the second floor. The chimney from the Keeping Room fireplace ran behind the staircase wall. The paint is the original color—a glaze of gray-green over yellow. In about 1820, all the houses in Litchfield were painted a fashionable off-white, and it was only by chemical analysis that the original paint colors were discovered.

Not surprisingly, the house was extended over the years. A two-story south wing was added in the eighteenth century, a barrel porch containing the original front-door pediment arrived at the beginning of the nineteenth, an east-wing kitchen came in the second half of the nineteenth century, closely followed by a turret, and that century came to a close with the addition of a third story for the south wing—the so-called ballroom—with a number of windowseats set beneath leaded-glass windows.

The Keeping Room is home to the discreet brass plaque that designates the house a National Historic Landmark, an honor granted thanks to the purity of the house's architecture and detail, and to its having been built by a Signatory to the Declaration of Independence. Only two or three such plaques are to be found in private homes in Connecticut. The owners of Wolcott's house are justly proud of having one of them in theirs.

But they also take pride in the way they have recreated a small part of the most glorious period of American history. Their recreation has given them an escape from the technology-obsessed twentieth century to a more gracious, leisurely age, when ordinary men could still accomplish great things. As the owner says, "We live in a historic landmark... perhaps we are similar to a chipmunk fortunate enough to live in a grand oak tree. One can feel pleased and proud of it without claiming credit."

LEFT:
A freestanding bathtub with claw feet stands in the center of the 1920s-style bathroom. Plumbing would have been introduced to the house in the nineteenth century.

ABOVE, RIGHT, AND BELOW LEFT:
The bedrooms have all been decorated in a lighter, early nineteenth-century style, with areas of pale paint on the walls enlivened by the use of contrasting colors on baseboards and beams.

The wind-scoured clapboards on the Maine farmhouse bear witness to their original owner's apparent status: typically, the narrower the clapboards, the finer the millwork—thus, a greater investment in material and labor. Nine-over-six windows are typical of Colonial construction. Until it could be fabricated by machine, glass was rare and costly, so windowpanes, by necessity, were small. Like the roof, the lean-to behind the house is shingled.

# MAINE CHANCE

For many residents of New England and points farther south, the "land of the pointed firs"—as Maine's beloved author Sarah Orne Jewett described her native state—offers an escape worth every minute of the effort it takes to get there. "Down East" benefits from the longest coastline of any of the original Colonies —almost 300 rock-strewn miles as the crow flies—with a climate moderated by the warm current of the Gulf Stream. Abundant forests stretch over the border into Canada; homesteads, therefore, like the down-to-earth farmstead featured here, are, quite naturally, made of wood. Like its Colonial counterparts, too, the house is forthright and austere. In summary, it is shelter: pure and simple.

E ndowed with Yankee thrift seasoned by laconic humor, Down Easterners hold themselves in taciturn reserve, especially regarding "summer people." Ask for directions, even to Maine's world-famous retailer L.L. Bean, and you are likely to encounter a succinct "You can't get there from here."

Representative of Down East reticence is a farmhouse that stands abreast a hill under the sheltering canopy of a decades-old sugar maple. Sheathed in clapboards that have weathered to a soft pewter gray, the shingle-roofed dwelling once housed a family that may have been more educated and well-to-do than its neighbors. An evocative hint is offered by the front door: instead of being

ABOVE:
The ladderback rocker with its original splint seat is a classic example of Shaker craftsmanship.

RIGHT:
In the kitchen, Shaker ingenuity manifests itself in architectural details such as the pegboard that girdles the room and the shelf that drops from the ceiling to hold an array of bowls. Shaker furnishings mix companionably with pieces of a more primitive mien, such as the farm table with scrubbed-pine top.

The Shakers arrived in America just two years prior to the Declaration of Independence, in 1774, and spread, in less than fifty years, to nineteen communities that ranged from nearby Canterbury, Maine, all the way to Pleasant Hill, Kentucky.

LEFT:
Architectural trim on the main floor—including the plain, but formal mantel in the living room—is painted barn-red, a color that early settlers and Shakers alike both adored. Although they lived apart from the world, the Shakers were astute in business; nor were they immune to design influences from "outside." A bentwood rocker exemplifies this interest: inspired by Art Nouveau prototypes, it is distinguished by a Shaker-style woven-tape back and seat.

ABOVE LEFT:
Bright blue milk paint highlights a side door with storm-door mate.

RIGHT AND ABOVE RIGHT:
A glance down an enfilade of rooms leads past a stately procession of cupboards and blanket chests to a kick-scuffed door painted robin's-egg blue.

## THE SHAKERS BELIEVED FERVENTLY IN A LIFE EXEMPLIFIED BY THEIR MOST FAMOUS HYMN: "TIS A GIFT TO BE SIMPLE." THE FARMHOUSE IS EXACTLY THAT, AND, THUS, IS PERFECT, TOO.

trimmed out, like the windows, in plain casings, it is framed by pilasters and capped with a lintel, a conceit echoing Greek temple construction—an idea brought back to America from France by Thomas Jefferson. Chimneys at each end of the main structure attest to the center-hall plan, which supplanted center-chimney plans of an earlier era.

From the lawn, the house yields no clue to its interiors, which, as it happens, serenely fuse Colonial and Shaker design. Devoted to the pursuit of perfection as an expression of their faith, the Shakers (so-named for a stylized dance) believed fervently in a life exemplified by their most famous hymn: "Tis a Gift to be Simple." The farmhouse is exactly that, and, thus, to its owner, is perfect, too.

ABOVE:
A frame Laura studded with buttons rests alongside old family photos on the dining room mantelpiece.

RIGHT:
Even window sashes present opportunities to display prized auction finds.

MAIN PICTURE:
The dining room (seen through door) occupies the original section of the house, a 1700s stone structure that contained only this downstairs room and a garret above. Laura and Richard changed the direction of the main staircase in the "new," 1850s part of the house; in so doing, they blocked off an access to the cellar, saving its door to panel a recess now used as a seat.

# MEETING HOUSE

When a meeting of minds evolves into a marriage of souls, harmony reigns. A Pennsylvania farmhouse, transformed into a weekend getaway by architectural designer Laura Bohn and her husband, builder Richard Fiore, perfectly realizes this ideal. The dwelling also respects and mirrors the minimalist philosophy of its first owners, a Quaker couple who sealed their union with the planting of two maple trees in front of the house—trees Laura and Richard tend, like the house, with loving care.

OPPOSITE:
**Doors from the dining room lead into a pair of parlors, one of which houses the couple's pool table. Laura designed the chandelier to cast a halo over a table she had made from rough-cut cedar; the tabletop measures 60 inches across.**

ABOVE RIGHT:
**Laura fashioned a lamp from a 1920s silverplate trophy — won at bridge.**

BELOW RIGHT:
**Art and mirrors lean against walls, to be moved around as the mood strikes.**

ABOVE:
**In the kitchen foyer, a dry sink dating from the 1850s acts as an impromptu telephone stand for the old rotary dialer; louvered shutters filter sunlight.**

LEFT:
**On the pebbled patio, two separate sets of wrought-iron garden chairs join a parson's bench around another of Laura's generously scaled tables. The top lifts off the sawbuck base, which folds up so the unit can be stored inside during the winter.**

T he rolling landscape that lies just west of the Delaware River, which divides New Jersey and Pennsylvania, is as benign a terrain as one would wish for a weekend escape. An easy drive from Manhattan, Bucks County has long been associated with the Quakers, a gentle folk who eschew war and worship together in silent accord. One of their leaders, William Penn, established nearby Philadelphia, as well as the state that bears his name.

Even though the Quakers are best known for their staunch defense of peace, their subdued taste in dress and their chaste, unpretentious homes have also earned a measure of respect, especially from those in the world of design. It was this sense of dignity and order that first attracted Laura Bohn and Richard Fiore to the farmhouse. Although the place had subsided into a state of neglect, it—and an adjacent dairy barn—projected an aura of calm that was the antidote to the couple's hectic life in New York. That the house posed a series of structural challenges was not an issue; they could see that it had good "bones."

Once basic services were restored, the couple began the task of bringing the old spaces back to life; they also decided to add on a sunny new kitchen wing. From start to finish, the renovation

THIS PAGE:
With its wall of glass, the new kitchen recalls summer kitchens of the past. The airy interior opens to a 12-foot-high roofline; locally quarried lilac granite covers the floor. The three-by-eight-foot zinc-topped island is paneled on the back; drawers, instead of shelves and doors, eliminate the hassle of reaching for pots and lids.

OPPOSITE:
When they added the kitchen, the couple left a window to the dining room, which looks into the breakfast alcove (main picture). The cupboard, from Virginia, wears its original coat of paint—inside and out—in one of Laura's favorite colors: taupe. Open shelving backs up against windows, which allow light through.

LEFT:
As elsewhere in the house, the master bedroom plays host to a comfortable mix of furnishings. Laura designed the bed: she built out the wall behind to hold his-and-hers bookcases, then attached duplicate runs of crown molding along the ceiling to anchor the rods that hold the linen bedhangings. A luxurious touch: two grand, draped tables that flank the bed. Lamps on each are overscaled, too, but made of glass so they do not overwhelm the still-lifes they are meant to enhance.

RIGHT:
Laura sponge-painted walls in the hall to bring out the plaster's rough texture. Richard built the cupboard to fit the niche.

BELOW RIGHT:
A sheep portrait by Richard's daughter, Johanna, hangs above a blanket chest.

## THE RENOVATION WAS A SHARED ADVENTURE—FROM DECIDING WHAT TYPE OF PANELING WOULD GO WHERE, TO MIXING COLORS, TO HUNTING FOR JUST THE RIGHT ANTIQUES AND ACCESSORIES TO FURNISH EACH ROOM.

was a shared adventure—from deciding what type of paneling would go where, to mixing colors for the architectural trim, to hunting for just the right antiques and accessories to furnish each room.

While the collaboration expresses the couple's less-is-more attitude toward design, it also reflects their respect for the original Quaker desire for balance and harmony. The best of the past—such as the pumpkin-pine floors and walk-in fireplace in the dining room—blends seamlessly with up-to-date amenities, such as the huge grill inset in the kitchen island, which was rescued from a defunct restaurant. Over time, even the new has acquired a rich patina, forming a comfortable backdrop for an ever-evolving collection of objects found at auction and others Laura and Richard have made themselves. The farmhouse is an active retreat, and a happy one.

# RUSTIC
## BEAUTY

ogs and the trees from which they are hewn are the closest most of us come to embracing the wild. For those who love the outdoors, there is nothing quite as satisfying as the aroma of wood smoke, be it from an open fire or from an indoor hearth. For true aficionados, that scent is only matched by the act of splitting a log. When ax meets wood, and the two halves of the log fall away from each other, the cleft between them cracks with the call of true escape. Wrested from the forest, logs also signify might, and a resolute taming of nature, so it is no wonder, then, that one of America's mythical heroes is Paul Bunyan, a titan of a lumberjack. Logs, too, rekindle the romance of the sturdy little cabin weathering the elements—especially as exemplified by the humble, hallowed birthplace of revered president Abraham Lincoln. Nostalgia for an equally noble, elemental connection to America's heritage motivated a resurgence in log construction that was spearheaded by some of the most powerful entrepreneurs of America's late-nineteenth-century Gilded Age. Devotees masterminded enormous camps and lodges of log and stone as havens of escape, then outfitted and decorated them with furnishings crafted from branch, bark, and twig. Today, log homes are built by the thousands in every region of the United States, many from kits that pop together as easily as that childhood toy, aptly named Lincoln Logs.

The plot on which the main house of this Great Camp is found covers one-and-a-half acres and revels in 485 feet of Long Lake shoreline. The house was built in 1908 from stone and wood—traditional Adirondack building materials. Located in the northwest of the Adirondack Mountains (the least developed part), lake and house stand in wondrous forest—giant spruce, white pine, maples, and silver birch. The camp was originally built for a family from Maryland. Their annual trek from home, with their servants and their silver (summer life in the Adirondack Mountains was quite a grand affair for such people), would have taken two full days, some of it over rough terrain. Indeed, it was those very "robber barons"—the people who built the summer camps in the Adirondacks —who brought the railroad to upstate New York to facilitate their summer migrations.

# TURN-OF-THE-CENTURY TRADITION

Deep in the Adirondack Mountains, the owner of a Great Camp packed with hunting memorabilia and family heirlooms carries on old traditions. Summer hospitality is organized with the same care and precision that the original mistress of the house expected. In other respects, too, the first owners would probably recognize the summer life of their old home.

RIGHT AND BELOW:
**The Great Room is a perfect 25-foot cube, heated by a massive fire with a granite surround. The gallery is original and leads to four bedrooms upstairs. Other features include the many mounted moose and deer heads and some lovely pieces of family furniture. The color taupe, used for the upholstery and the rug, predominates, but the pine beadboard has been left natural.**

TOP:
**The plentiful supply of wood in the Adirondacks made it one of the main building materials for the camps, as here, in the boathouse.**

ABOVE AND RIGHT:
**As the camps are solely for summer use, the covered porch is one of the most important rooms. Here, the owner–designer used her signature color—taupe—to paint the tongue-and-groove paneling of the porch and its wicker furniture. The furniture is original to the house, but the gauze screens are replacements.**

W hen she was a child, the owner of this magnificent stone and wood camp in the Adirondack Mountains spent many a blissful summer in the region, walking, boating, and picnicking. Yearning for a haven from her busy life as a textile designer in New York, she realized that such a haven existed in those mountains, along with her still-fresh childhood memories.

When a large part of one Great Camp—the main house, one of the boathouses, and the ice house—came on the market, she promptly bought it, complete with its length of shoreline, turn-of-the-century decor, and stuffed animal heads. The camp, with its mountain backdrop and stupendous views over the lake, has proved the perfect place for the owner and her friends to find rest and relaxation.

This camp is relatively small, compared to the grandiose scale of many from its era. It has only thirteen rooms. In addition to these and the boathouse and ice house purchased with them, the camp also had a laundry, caretaker's cottage, tennis court, lean-to shed, and a second boathouse.

The main thing the owner did when she purchased the camp was to clean. Woodwork was washed and repainted, floors refinished, and appliances replaced. But the first owners would still recognize the house, with its Great Room, dining room, kitchen, butler's pantry, porch, bedroom, and bathroom on the ground floor, and its four bedrooms and two bathrooms upstairs.

Just a little furniture came with the house— including an unusual antler chandelier, which has become something of a talking point. Most of the

OPPOSITE:
**Like the Great Room, the dining room is heated by a fireplace made from local granite. A set of Mies van der Rohe chairs accompanies the family heirloom table, and a contemporary plexiglass and chrome light fixture hangs overhead. The sideboard, restored to a warm honey color, came with the house.**

ABOVE:
**A quilt in the owner's signature taupe, and a pair of bronze stools in classical Greek style with woven leather seats, bring a touch of elegance to the old pine wall paneling of the master bedroom.**

TOP LEFT, ABOVE LEFT, AND RIGHT:
**The camp's kitchen and bathrooms retain their calm simplicity, with wood flooring and painted tongue-and-groove paneling. In the kitchen, country chairs are hung, Shakerlike, from a rail, while a bathroom is adorned with one more stuffed head—a reminder of the days when the camp was a center for hunting, shooting, and fishing.**

rest is antique, much of it family pieces. The dining-room table, for instance, has been in the owner's family for five generations.

The early days of the Adirondack camps included many formal events, the sort of occasion described by writers such as Henry James and Edith Wharton. The present owner loves to keep up those traditions whenever she entertains. Weekend visits include a compulsory "dress-up" night, and birthday parties are evening-dress affairs. There are less formal occasions, too, such as lunch on the porch or dinner served on the dock by the lakeside.

In bygone days, too, despite the formality, Adirondack camp life was strictly regulated by nature. Then, as now, on the shores of Long Lake, toward the end of August, the evenings become cool, and the fires in the Great Room and the dining room have to be maintained constantly or it is impossible to heat the large building. The summer people gradually pack up their things and return to their everyday lives, while the great houses settle down to their winter slumber. Their owners are ready once again to face the onslaught of city life. Just as in the first days of the camps, the Adirondacks continue to weave their calming magic.

**ABOVE AND LEFT:**
The ice house has painted clapboard walls and a jaunty diamond-shaped window in its side extension. The extension was probably added as a children's playroom.

**MAIN PICTURE:**
With vast areas of the Adirondacks to choose from, early pioneers could virtually pick their own lake or mountain near which to build a home. While some decided to build close to their friends, others went in search of pristine wilderness. In the early days, before the advent of the railroads, the only access to the camps was by water, so boats were an essential part of camp life. Today, old docks, boathouses, and boats are still an important part of the escape, allowing modern escapees to feel something of the pioneering spirit.

FAR LEFT:
Birds flock to this quiet spot. The family grills the fish they catch in the lake.

LEFT AND OPPOSITE BELOW RIGHT:
The main house of the camp dates from about 1900, and has recently had a formal staircase to the door and veranda added. It is one of six buildings that made up the original property.

OPPOSITE, ABOVE:
The family have known the waters of this huge and unpopulated lake in Maine since 1946.

OPPOSITE, BELOW LEFT:
The sauna, which also has a fine view of the lake, is built of rough logs like the house. A "no hunting" sign is not simply a joke: hunting is strictly controlled in the area.

The American wilderness holds huge lakes, acres of dense forest, and towering mountains—once the hunting grounds of Native Americans and, later, the solitary preserves of trappers, pioneer farmers, and hunters. Paul and Melba Chodosh discovered their own patch of wilderness as long ago as 1946. Their lovely old house is a full day's drive from their present apartment in Lower Manhattan, but that does not deter them. In fact, in New York all winter, they pine for its solitude and long for the advent of spring to bring them back.

# REMOTE LOG CABIN

The holding is in Maine on the shore of a long, active lake. The area teems with moose and bear, birds and fish. Mel says it has been "a long love affair." They first found the area in 1946 and went back to visit regularly until, in 1963, they bought the camp that has been their family home ever since. The house was built in the early twentieth century entirely by hand from spruce logs, which were also peeled by hand and put into place with a pulley, horses, and manpower. It must have been a very hard life because it gets extremely cold in winter: −30°F (−34°C). The lake freezes solid, and a nearby hotel still cuts ice from the lake to cool the icehouse where they store food.

This primitive house in a wilderness has taken over the lives of Paul and Mel because it has become an integral part of the family. The simple building has seen the arrival of their five children, and, latterly, their eleven grandchildren. "It's a focal point for family gatherings, children, husbands, wives, and their children. It's a very major part of our lives. It's what we're really all about."

Since Paul retired, they have spent more time here than ever. This is just as well, because the couple seem to spend a great deal of their time entertaining at this lovely old house. All their children and grandchildren visit when they can, and can be accommodated quite easily. If there are too many to fit into the house, they put up tents in the

OPPOSITE AND TOP LEFT:
**Log-cabin construction has been used for the inner walls of the wide veranda. It looks out over the lake and is a perfect setting for family parties.**

TOP RIGHT:
**The chairs on the veranda are well worn and comfortable, with cushions in bleached cotton; while tables, chairs, and table lamps seem to be made from local driftwood and branches with their bark left on.**

RIGHT AND ABOVE:
**Wood is the main fuel here, and along with open fires, the house has wood-burning stoves, like this one in the sauna. A cut-tin lantern casts shadows on the wall at night.**

woods and on the lakeside. They haven't run out of space yet. All major family reunions take place beside the lake. Mel says, "It's a wonderful place for entertaining. The main porch will fit a hundred people standing. We have buffet meals there, and though there is electricity, we use candles at night."

The whole area is under a preservation order that stipulates that the lake should be kept as wild as it was when the Norridgewick Indians hunted its shores. "Our lake is very large, and when we first moved here its shores were unpopulated. We first rented a cottage in an American Plan Camp. The fishing was good and, though we didn't fish at first, we learned to. The place was so peaceful and back-to-nature—it made an absolute change from our daily lives. There was the opportunity to garden. Then we were able to teach the children things that were impossible in the city—they became boatsmen, they learned to swim and practice the simple life. They could see the stars without bright city lights."

There has been some development around the lake, but the area is still remote and wild. Moose, bear, deer, peregrine falcons, and bald eagles are

ABOVE:
**Mel is a potter. This bowl of hers is shown off on a table with tiles also made by her.**

RIGHT AND TOP:
**It can get extremely cold on the lakeside in winter, and a log fire (supplemented by efficient heating) draws the family to the old hearth. Stairs lead to the bedrooms, while duck decoys, old rifles, and rubble-stone walls recreate the feel of traditional log-cabin life.**

all found in the area. The Chodoshes love living in this wild country. "Black bear were seen often years ago because there were open areas for garbage dumps. When those went, they went. Now the bears are coming back again—no one can understand why. They are not really dangerous unless you come between a cub and its mother, or remove their food. Then they can even come into your house if they get hungry."

So the wilderness out in Maine is quite real, and beyond the lake the high mountains create a rugged backdrop. The lake itself provides fish for their meals; it contains landlocked salmon and rainbow trout, which the family catch and grill for themselves—no one is allowed to sell them.

The love affair is by no means over. "There are so few people here, and we can't even see our neighbor's house. It's truly idyllic, a make-believe place. The world isn't this way any more. We feel extremely grateful and privileged to be here, and every day we thank whoever made it happen."

> WE WERE ABLE TO TEACH THE CHILDREN THINGS THAT WERE IMPOSSIBLE IN THE CITY—THEY BECAME BOATSMEN, THEY LEARNED TO SWIM AND PRACTICE THE SIMPLE LIFE. THEY COULD SEE THE STARS WITHOUT BRIGHT CITY LIGHTS.

ABOVE:
An old-fashioned freestanding tub almost completely fills the bathroom —it had to be shoehorned in. The walls are all planked, and the shower might well have come from the nineteenth century.

RIGHT:
This bedroom is typical of the house. Every wall, floor, and ceiling is covered in tongue-and-groove beadboard from the local forests, all left natural, while the sharply angled ceiling recalls a roof ready to shed inches of snow. The barley-twist wooden bed, country chair, plain wool blanket, and rag rug would all be at home in a pioneer's cabin.

ABOVE LEFT:
Like a fairytale castle, the North Star lodge is "moated"—but with decking rather than water. Railings are filled in with near-invisible mesh; infilling is required to prevent anyone falling off. The house is constructed entirely of untreated pine logs from "standing-dead" trees. The advantage of using such wood is two-fold: Removing standing-dead trees is an environmentally friendly gesture, and the logs are already seasoned, not green.

ABOVE RIGHT:
Hoopback chaises made from branches found on the property enjoy a long view down the valley.

OPPOSITE:
Steeply pitched roofs are accented at their peaks with cross-pieces that resemble skis—or the poles poking out the tops of teepees.

# ROCKY MOUNTAIN RETREAT For a family longing to get away from it all, not just any off-the-beaten-track place would do. It had to be located near a prime ski resort, but one that had plenty going on during the summer as well. And the home they envisioned had to be nothing more nor less than a lodge, one inspired not only by the Great Camps of the Adirondacks, but also by the grand hotels built by the National Park Service in the time-honored tradition of the American West—of logs culled from local forestlands.

The Colorado Rockies are home to two world-renowned ski resorts, Aspen and Vail. Both can be reached by automobile, or by planes, which weave through mountain chasms before alighting at the wide-open valleys and ski slopes that distinguish the high snow country. Both, too, are surrounded by far-reaching land holdings set aside by the federal government to be "forever wild": one of these, the North Star Nature Preserve, provides the backdrop for the family hideaway pictured here.

Like the hotels that overlook treasured natural wonders such as the Grand Canyon, this generously scaled homestead takes advantage of a spectacular

OPPOSITE:
On the slope-side of the house, a mini-grove of delicate aspen trees sheds its distinctive heart-shaped leaves; as these fade from green to yellow, they shine like bangles in the sun.

RIGHT:
Interior spaces reveal the myriad uses of wood and their varying degrees of finish, from bark-covered to sanded and waxed.

ABOVE:
Three dozen steps climb four levels to reach the back entrance to the house. Railings display the hairy texture of partially peeled bark.

LEFT, RIGHT, AND FAR RIGHT:
The influence of Adirondack camps is most evident in the stickwork that embellishes fireplace surrounds and chimneybreasts. Patterns range from simple lozenges to complex basketweave designs. To protect against excess heat buildup, the fireboxes are prefabricated units, which contain high-rated insulation.

ABOVE:
A toothy spiral stair leads up to bedrooms; the thick wooden slabs used as steps still bear traces of bark.

LEFT:
The Great Room soars to a majestic system of roof trusses composed of robust logs of Bunyanesque proportions. The trusses are supported by tree trunks of elephantine girth. The effect of the whole is awe-inspiring—but is mitigated by pools of cozy furnishings that invite the homeowners and their friends to gather together to converse, dine, and bask in the streaming rays of the sun.

RIGHT:
One of the two "host" shield-back dining chairs that stand at the head and foot of the dining table shows off its spiky topknot. Every chair's willow back has the comfortable "give" of a rubber band.

view; it also enjoys the privacy that only a protected swath of public land can provide. But the property faced the challenge of a mountainous terrain: a steep slope. Designer Holly Lueders saw this as an opportunity—to build up and out so the house would feel connected to the outdoors on every level.

Logs for the house were all felled with an eye to preserving the environment; most are so-called "standing-dead" trees culled from stands of forest that had been scorched by fires in Wyoming's Yellowstone Park. Fire is nature's way of revitalizing her forests; smoke also disinfects the logs, ridding them of insects. Lueders made her selection based on function, reserving the longest, largest, and straightest trunks for columns and beams, and logs of lesser girth—in graduated sizes—for ceiling trusses and walls. Branches collected on the property were transformed into ancillary architectural accents and furnishings as diverse as stair rails, chandeliers, and bedsteads.

As a tribute to traditional American log homes, Lueders cemented the peeled-log walls with chinking, but, instead of a pioneer mix of horsehair and plaster, she worked with a twenty-first-century polymer, which is elastic enough to allow logs to expand and contract naturally in response to the temperature.

Indoors, Lueders opened the ceiling in the Great Room comprising the living and dining areas to the full height of the roof. A colonnade of immense logs strides the length of the room and supports a vast ceiling-framing system of exposed log trusses.

Energy efficiency is an issue in a dry climate with extremes in temperature; here, wide expanses of thermal-pane glass repel intense cold, yet harness massive doses of sun. Furnishings, too, are warm, cozy, and inviting—no mean feat in rooms this large. Sofas are upholstered in velvet, or in remnants of kilim rugs, which also cover a loveseat, selected chairs and pillows, and benches. Beds are cozied with heavy spreads or down-filled comforters. In short, the house is a haven in every sense of the word.

Each of the bedrooms in the North Star lodge is furnished comfortably, but minimally, with the bare essentials. Each, too, showcases an ebullient collection of log-and-twig style furniture.

OPPOSITE ABOVE LEFT AND THIS PAGE:
These beds were fabricated from sinuous, wind-twisted branches that appear to grow directly out of the floor. The undulating forms stand out in sharp contrast to the regimental arrangement of the stacked wall-logs behind the beds. Some branches still bear twigs that might once have held nests in the woods outside.

OPPOSITE ABOVE RIGHT:
A four-poster bed is softened by a set of lace-edged, linen tab-top bed curtains.

OPPOSITE BELOW LEFT:
A twiggy lamp recalls an old-fashioned Texas oil derrick.

OPPOSITE BELOW RIGHT:
Another bed has a lyre-style headboard.

BRANCHES COLLECTED ON THE PROPERTY WERE TRANSFORMED INTO STAIR RAILS, CHANDELIERS, AND BEDSTEADS.

To find this camp on Lake Placid in northern New York State, you have to first find a village on Lake Placid, make your way to a marina, then cross by boat to an island. In a world where travel is becoming increasingly simple, there is still something of the pioneering spirit to be found in the Adirondacks, if only because the camps close down in September and don't open again until after Easter. Development of the camps started around 1872. Lake Placid was one of the first areas in the Adirondacks to witness them. During the next thirty years, over a hundred camps sprang up on the lake shore and its islands. The lake was known as "The Gem of the Adirondacks" and "Peerless Placid." This camp is perched precariously on the slopes of an island, with wonderful views from its terraces and boathouse over the lake, virgin forests, and mountain ranges.

# PLACID ISLAND HOME FROM HOME

The calm shores of Lake Placid, in northern New York State, play host to a lovingly rebuilt and lovingly used wooden Great Camp. Here, the modern-day owners—expatriates yearning for a sight of home, the natural successors to nineteenth-century industrialists hungry for the simple life—recapture childhood memories of idyllic summers spent swimming, boating, and picnicking.

In the United States, the late nineteenth and early twentieth centuries were a period of unprecedented urban development and economic growth, in which many prospered, but none more than the industrialists of New York. Families such as the Carnegies and the Vanderbilts, who amassed vast fortunes from boom industries such as steel, lumber, and the railroads, may have lived in the lap of luxury in their urban mansions, but still felt the need to escape the city environs.

This was something they achieved from the late 1880s on by constructing log-built lodges in the forests and mountains of the Adirondacks. Known as Great Camps, these rustic retreats drew their architectural inspiration from the log cabins of the early American pioneers, such as Davy Crockett, James Fenimore Cooper, and Daniel Boone, from the lumber and mining camps of the eighteenth and nineteenth centuries in the Adirondacks themselves, and from the log chalets of the European Alps.

For an expatriate couple, living in London, the urge to get away from city life and back to a simpler way of being—as experienced by the turn-of-the-century families before them—was becoming increasingly strong. This rundown place, tottering on its crumbling foundations on Buck Island, immediately seemed to be the answer.

In this massively forested region, the natural building material was wood, and the early builders developed a unique regional style. Wooden decks, walkways—including the long stairway up to the house from the boathouse—and terraces allow unsurpassed views of the natural surroundings. The original camps and lodges were modeled on frontier houses and reflected the desire of their wealthy owners to reconnect to a simple, self-sufficient, honest lifestyle.

When the owners are in the Adirondacks for their family break, one of the aims of their escape is to spend as much time as possible in "the great outdoors." They can do this without leaving the house, too. The property is well supplied with decks and terraces overlooking beautiful views—and plenty of comfortable chairs in which to sit and admire them.

**STRONG, SOLID, AND REMOTE, THE OLD CAMP ON LAKE PLACID WAS JUST CRYING OUT FOR LOVE, AFFECTION, AND A BIG HAPPY FAMILY TO BRING ITS GLOOMY, DILAPIDATED ROOMS BACK TO LIFE.**

Strong, solid, and remote—there is something of the pioneer about this island dwelling. The old camp on Lake Placid was just crying out for love, affection, and a big happy family to bring its gloomy, dilapidated rooms back to life. It found all this and more in the husband and wife who bought it on a wing and a prayer. It was crumbling and unmortgageable, but had plenty of potential.

In her childhood, the wife spent a part of each summer on a small lake and some time in the Adirondacks. She cherishes memories of swimming, boating, hiking, and just living the outdoor life. Her Danish husband loves boats and boating, and similarly yearned for a life without any hint of glitz, one that would hark back to sunlit summers and the open air. And since they live abroad, they both wanted a place where they could have their families and friends to stay for as long as possible.

They knew they could find all this at Lake Placid, but it would have to be just a house for the summer, for in winter the lake freezes over. In late

fall, the last of the blazing autumn foliage dropping from the trees marks the end of their idyllic retreat until summer of the next year.

But to enjoy any idyllic summers there, like the wealthy New Yorker families who had first discovered and developed the Adirondacks, they had some major structural problems to address. These problems included the foundations. The house had to be lifted, have new foundations established, and then set down square again. During this painful process, the owners discovered rotten walls that simply had to be torn down. But out of this necessary evil came good. Now, instead of the numerous small rooms bequeathed to them by the original design, they can enjoy open, unobstructed spaces, totally at one with the feel of the lake.

Finally, they have just what they wanted in this restored vacation house on Peerless Placid: A warm, welcoming home that can sleep a multitude and which, they hope, will stand the test of time, providing many happy lakeside summers for their children and their children's children.

THIS PAGE:
Simple furniture adorns the deck of the house so meals can be taken alfresco.

ABOVE LEFT:
With its narrower boards and smaller window, the top bedroom is part of the original old camp.

BELOW LEFT:
By contrast, the master bedroom is light and airy with doors leading onto the terrace. The interior is simple and uncluttered, enjoying glimpses of the mountains and lakes on all sides.

LEFT:
The little cabin shares the lawn with a shed the Shopes use to store bee-keeping equipment. During thunderstorms, the Shope kids take bets on how often lightning will strike the rooftop lightning rod.

ABOVE:
The Shopes dug a four-foot-deep crawl space underneath the foundation that supports the cabin, then faced the foundation wall with stones from the clearing. Four trees from the property serve as porch columns.

## BACKWOODS CABIN

For Allan Shope, escape meant but one thing: a cabin in the woods. Like Henry David Thoreau, he sought a spot with soul, a place to root his family in nature and the simple life. Plot by plot, he proceeded to purchase enough forestland to achieve his dream: a thousand acres of pine and cedar intermingled with black birch, hemlock, oak, and apple. Located along the border shared by New York State and Connecticut, where he maintains an architectural practice, the land encloses a long valley and foothills with a view to the Catskills a hundred miles away.

LEFT:
The kitchen and a bathroom tuck into the left and right of the chimney.

RIGHT:
All furnishings but the dining table—which is authentic—are reproductions of Gustav Stickley's Arts & Crafts designs. Gridded windows are also inspired by Craftsman models.

OPPOSITE:
The Shopes fabricated the rustic cedar fireplace surround right on the spot. A bedtime ritual for each of the children is to place a burning ember in the mouth of one of the dragon andirons on their way up to the sleeping loft.

Another, equally compelling motivation for the forestland was Allan's desire to design his cabin using local materials; he also wanted to build it with his own hands, with the help of his family. After he and his wife had settled on the perfect spot, they and a few friends cleared the site themselves, amassing all the lumber necessary, as well as stones, which would face the foundation wall and chimney. "Every piece of wood and every stone came from within 100 yards of the house—just the distance we could manage," he says. Only the four massive hunks of granite used for the fireplace (and the brick) had to be trucked in, but even they came from a quarry located nearby.

Allan's design concept for the family getaway was as clear-cut as the logs he began to refine on the portable sawmill he set up near the new foundation. It would be, in essence, a one-room structure that would appear humble and unassuming on the outside and uplifting within. The architectural conceit he came up with to accomplish this was inspired: he decided to cap his dwelling with a pyramidal roof with intersecting rafters that would foster the illusion that it rises higher than its actual dimensions decree.

He also wanted to set up what he calls "awesome contrasts" in scale, texture, and light. Inside and

THIS PAGE:
After they had gathered all the cedar branches they needed for the railings for the double stair and balcony overlook, the Shope children told their Dad exactly how to cut them and where they wanted him to nail each piece. He let them do a lot of nailing, too; "you should see the nail patterns they made," he says with pride.

OPPOSITE:
Allan Shope designed the three-foot-wide, three-foot-deep entry to be deliberately claustrophobic—and to make it feel "as if you are exploding into the wide open space of the big room." One wall collects books; the other (not seen) displays nature trophies picked up by the children. Truncated twigs are great for hanging hats.

OPPOSITE:
The rhythm of the windows follows that of the rafters. Two-foot-deep benches under windows provide extra seating as well as storage.

ABOVE:
Additional storage hides behind wallboards.

RIGHT:
One chunk of log becomes a newel post.

FAR RIGHT:
It took Allan and his friends four days to erect the ceiling. Converging extra-narrow rafters make the ceiling appear higher than its 25 feet; thin furring strips reinforce the illusion.

out, the roof appears at once intimate and vast; inside, the rhythm and composition of its structural members appears both jazzy and still, like a Shaker basket—or a weaving. Allan comes from a family of weavers, so he wanted the roof to demonstrate visibly the basic "warp and weft" of that homey craft.

The entire family, as well as friends, got into the act. The Shopes' children all helped with nailing; they also selected the cedar branches for the railings along the stairs and sleeping loft. "We had a wonderful time doing it together," Allan says.

In the years since the cabin was completed in 1996, the Shopes have expanded the house with a small, separate bedroom addition, because it turned out that the cabin proved irresistible to three bats, whose flight patterns disturbed Allan's wife. But, the new space comes with its own attic, so the kids can bounce back and forth depending on their mood for privacy—or how many friends come to stay.

**THE ROOF APPEARS AT ONCE INTIMATE AND VAST; INSIDE, THE RHYTHM OF ITS STRUCTURAL MEMBERS APPEARS BOTH JAZZY AND STILL, LIKE A SHAKER BASKET.**

With its cluster of agricultural buildings and its old farmhouse, Mildred's Place has lain undisturbed for most of the twentieth century. Its previous owner, Mildred, lived here for over eighty years and made no changes in that time. But when the time came for the estate to be sold, there was a new generation of escapees waiting in the wings. Reached by a long track through the woods, the estate nestles in a small valley bounded by woods and hills. It seems a world away from New York City where its present owners

work. While they intend to gently put their mark on this idyllic spot, they are determined to retain its integrity and the simple way of life that was lived here over many years. Their only real addition is the Guest Tent—and though Mildred drew her water from a spring and stored it in jars in a sort of cave under the house, the new owners have drilled a well. They have also installed electricity in some parts of the house. Despite these changes, the spirit of the house remains as true and steady as ever.

THIS PAGE TOP RIGHT, OPPOSITE BELOW LEFT AND RIGHT:
As its name suggests, the Guest Tent is the place where weekend visitors stay. The bed that now graces it was found at the top of Mildred's House and brought down, in triumph. The Guest Tent backs onto the woods. It requires a guest of a certain mettle to lie in Mildred's old bed, listening to the cries of the coyotes and wondering if, by any chance, there's going to be a visit from a big, black bear.

# REFUGE FOR A RURAL SOUL

Deep in the ancient forests near the Delaware River, a collection of wooden farm buildings makes the perfect escape from modernity for four artistic people. These humble dwellings, hardly altered since the nineteenth century, are truly in harmony with the natural world they inhabit.

For over eighty years, since she had been brought there as a baby by her parents, a fine old lady called Mildred lived on this 90-acre estate in northern Pennsylvania near the Delaware River. There was no electricity, and she drew water from a natural spring. Mildred was one of that happy breed of privileged human beings who are completely at home in the natural world.

The property is now owned by a clothes designer and her partner, an entomologist and conceptual artist. This sophisticated pair worked in New York, but yearned for the simple life. Mildred's Place, set in woodland amid rolling countryside, suits them perfectly. But, above all, Mildred's Place embodies humility and solid values, and this was part of what they were seeking. The search for somewhere that was more than a chichi getaway was what also led two artist friends to join in this really big farm adventure. The four are a spirited pioneering band.

Since they arrived, they have made some changes, but, apart from converting the abandoned agricultural buildings into basic dwellings—they call it "adaptive reuse"—their changes are relatively superficial. Their aim is to make Mildred's Place habitable, but to leave as much as possible alone.

The house was sold with its furniture. Restoration was kept to a minimum, and any additions are either old pieces inherited by the designer, or objects found in flea markets or thrift stores. As far as possible, the present-day owners want to feel as if they are gently shuffling in Mildred's footsteps.

TOP:
**Mildred's House.**

ABOVE:
**The Red Hut (the privy) still sits behind Mildred's House. It has always been attractively decorated, inside and out.**

RIGHT:
**The second-floor veranda attached to Mildred's House seems to lean precariously into the valley, so that this table's front legs have to be propped up on bricks. All the original paintwork is in the muted colors typical of the late nineteenth century.**

ABOVE:
The canvas wallcovering downstairs in Mildred's House was installed to provide insulation. It is the only room in the house to have it. Painted a vibrant blue in the early twentieth century, the present owners have refrained from repainting it. The contrasting wooden battens keep the canvas in place but are also decorative. Mildred would still feel at home here, among her furniture.

LEFT:
The Horse Shed makes a comfortable, candlelit home.

OPPOSITE AND TOP:
The Horse Shed, with its new pine siding, deep-buttoned sofa, and fruitwood rocker, is where the designer likes to sketch, drink her morning coffee, and make business calls. One side is open, screened from the summer sun by a simple, looped-up canvas awning. An old washstand and basin are the only washing facilities here.

ABOVE FAR LEFT:
Indoor dining—only in bad weather.

ABOVE LEFT:
The Barn's sitting area is protected from the elements by a canvas tarpaulin. The painted trunk was found, full of old family letters, in the chicken coop.

ABOVE RIGHT:
In the kitchen, there are no cabinets or refrigerator, so produce is bought from the local shops and every household item is on view.

ABOVE FAR RIGHT:
This bed, in the Barn, was found on the property, while the quilt and other fabrics were found in the owner's grandmother's attic in Georgia. The wooden slats of the walls and roof keep off most of the rain.

The Horse Shed, converted from a stable, is the place where the designer and her partner sleep and relax. It has no electricity, but has been covered with new pine boards, each one—in true Mildred spirit— sawn and nailed in place by the designer herself.

The late-nineteenth-century two-up two-down farmhouse—Mildred's House—has been left much as it was, with its original eccentric canvas wallcovering and its gaudy paintwork. Downstairs is gradually being transformed into a library of books on art, history, philosophy, design, and natural history—subjects that reflect the interests, the obsessions even, of the four inhabitants.

Wishing to stay true to Mildred's spirit, they have decided to preserve the Red Hut (the privy, then and now) just as it was in her time—interior painted green and pink, floor adorned with floral linoleum, and windows screened with fresh lace curtains.

The large, airy, wood-slatted Barn has now been taken over by the two artists, who have built a two-story wooden structure in its center. It does not enjoy any natural light, but it does provide them

The only new structure on the estate, if it can be called a structure, is the Guest Tent. This was created with the nomad in mind. Even its furniture has led a nomadic existence, much of it having started life in Mildred's House. The crib is a treecrib, the sort that farmers' wives hung from the trees as they worked in the fields. Lying awake in the tent, visitors can hear the sound of rain dripping onto the canvas from the surrounding hemlock, white pine, and ash trees.

with a bedroom above and a reading room below. The rest of the Barn is where the four inhabitants get together to sit, cook, and eat.

In this part of the property, perhaps more than anywhere else, the residents' needs come second to those of the building and the environment. The Barn is not completely waterproof, nor is it proof against bird and animal droppings. It also lacks electricity, but it would be anathema to the new owners to have power installed, or to close up the gaps between the wooden slats of the walls and roof. Instead, they make do, reading and going to bed by candlelight and stringing tarpaulins above vulnerable sitting and sleeping areas. The Barn may now be a dwelling, but its owners celebrate rather than try to disguise its agricultural origins.

For the four owners, Mildred's Place is an escape route into their idea of a perfect existence. In fact, the designer (who hails from a town in Georgia with a population of one thousand) has sold her metropolitan home. Once-a-week visits to the city are more than enough for this woman of rural soul.

**LEFT:**
The kitchen walls and doors are covered in atmospheric graffiti. Generations of campers painted and scrawled their names here, along with whorls and stars. Family and friends who helped restore the camp continued the tradition. The ceiling is hung with dozens of striped paper lanterns.

**RIGHT:**
Curved branches, found in the nearby woods, give the impression they are holding up this rough stone fireplace.

The USA has some of the last true wildernesses in the Western world. Alexandra Champalimaud, an interior designer, and her businessman husband Bruce can depart from one of the most urban landscapes on earth, New York City, and within an hour of leaving suburbia, find themselves in an untouched slice of nature, where the silence is overwhelming and nature is in control. Their rural Connecticut retreat is a revived summer camp—complete with lake, cabins, and bears in the forest.

# CONNECTICUT CAMP RESTORED

LEFT AND OPPOSITE:
The living-room floor, walls, and ceiling are pine. Some of the furniture has survived from the time when the place was a camp. Other furniture looks as though it was made by a pioneer working with bare branches, while pictures are propped on shelves more often than hung. One end of the living room leads to the main bedroom, while the other opens into a hall whose doors open onto a veranda.

Nowadays, it's possible to enjoy the wilderness—the brilliant stars undimmed by city lights, the silence of the forests broken by the eerie cries of nature's hunters and hunted, the soft lapping of the water—with the added bonus of central heating and air conditioning in summer.

Camp Kent, 30 years ago, was a place for children set beside the shores of a forested lake. Bruce found it when it was beginning to decline, but the owner was only prepared to sell to someone who would change the property minimally. Bruce could not resist this Connecticut corner, down a dirt road, but just two hours from Manhattan.

The whole group of buildings was in a pretty bad state, having weathered three decades of fierce storms and icy winters, but the position was superb. Alexandra Champalimaud says, "The crumbling camp buildings were removed, except for the five that had life in them. A compound was created around a big barn overhanging the lake, which had long served as the Camp Kent theater. This theater is now the soul of our retreat." The clapboard main house has eight bedrooms. There are also a guesthouse with a further two bedrooms and the Adirondack-style cabin that can hold another seven

ABOVE:
The main bedroom has been simply arranged and decorated. Generous windows provide wide views over the water. Colors in the house are soft and subtle—whites, creams, and off-whites.

ABOVE RIGHT AND TOP RIGHT:
Much of the furniture is painted in soft colors similar to the sun-bleached tones found in pioneer homes. Here a blue-green side table is set against the plain wood of the living-room walls, against which boating pictures are propped. Other tablescapes include an old fan, a lamp perched on a pile of books, and local finds such as pheasant feathers, a stag's antler, and an old Coca-Cola bottle.

guests. The whole is set in 15 acres of wilderness. It is not unknown for as many as 24 friends and family to meet here for a weekend away from it all.

During the restoration the couple were extremely careful not to lose any of the charm of this ancient group of buildings hidden down a track. The style could be described as simplified Adirondack, with, for example, a branch—bark and all—holding the shower curtain. And the lake is brought into the whole scheme by a long, planked dock where the kayak is moored and, in summer, lounging chairs are arrayed to take advantage of the view.

Their intense involvement in its magic and its purity has made the family determined to preserve this remote corner of Connecticut. Alexandra says, "It retains that children's summer-camp feeling that brings a smile to every face. The theater is the

OPPOSITE PAGE, LEFT:
There are lots of places to relax by the lake—both indoors and out —such as this hammock, casually slung between trees.

OPPOSITE PAGE, BELOW RIGHT:
One pleasure of living by a lake is the choice of hidden corners that can be adapted for alfresco meals. A table flanked by Adirondack chairs and topped by a cheerful blue-and-white gingham cloth fits neatly outside the kitchen door.

RIGHT:
The decking boat dock holds inviting wooden deck chairs.

ABOVE LEFT:
A whole array of waders and ice skates, rubber boots, and hats are lined up in the hall, under a suitably cheery welcome board.

LEFT:
Rough twigs from the surrounding forests, along with logs and bleached decking, create a rustic gazebo at the far end of the veranda that overlooks the lake.

LEFT:
Most of the rooms are lumber-clad with the planks arrayed horizontally, as in all the best log cabins. Indeed, the rooms are cubes of lumber with planked and beamed ceilings, and floors of yet more planks. None is painted.

RIGHT AND BELOW:
One feature of the house is the repeated use of rough but charmingly curved branches retrieved from the nearby woods. In a guest bedroom they prop up a shelf for books over the bed. In the bathroom, a branch decorates a narrow gap between the wooden walls of a bathtub and a shower.

## CAMP KENT RETAINS THAT CHILDREN'S SUMMER-CAMP FEELING THAT BRINGS A SMILE TO EVERY FACE. THE THEATER IS THE ULTIMATE PARTY BARN IN THE SUMMER AND A BROOM-HOCKEY OR PING-PONG ROOM ON FRIGID WINTER DAYS.

ultimate party barn in the summer and a broom-hockey or ping-pong room on frigid winter days."

Camp Kent has become a camp for all ages of the family and their friends, shared with abundant wildlife—beaver, otters, wild turkey, deer, eagles, hawks, ruffled grouse, and the occasional black bear or coyote—along with all the creatures of the New England woods. The lake holds bass and pike, along with freshwater shrimp and mussels.

Beyond the lake are the forests. "The woodlands, wetlands, and meadows provide us with all the pleasures of the four full seasons in the New England woods. While the fall colors are world famous, and early spring is a study in delicacy, most spectacular is the June explosion of pink mountain laurel on the hillsides that run down to the lake—except perhaps when the icy winter arrives quickly on a windless day, freezing the lake into a clear sheet of glass through which you can see to the bottom of the lake. Last year we enjoyed a spectacular, sunny afternoon skating across the top of this crystal aquarium."

# NEW
# FRONTIER
## SPIRIT

**E**very generation in America has witnessed a new frontier. In the seventeenth century, it was the forested wilderness that fringed the Atlantic coast; later it was the plains and deserts that stretched to the Rockies, and the land that bordered the Pacific. Once the entire nation had been mapped, the frontier turned inward, to the towns and cities that sprang up at junctions and crossings on America's ever-expanding network of railroads and highways. Finally, with astronaut Neil Armstrong's moonwalk, the frontier plunged outward, into space. Although not every American is an Armstrong, many have pushed the envelope—physically, personally, and psychologically. To many, border, boundary, and frontier are elastic terms—especially when conceived to measure the desire for escape from the humdrum and everyday. As pioneers, Americans created dwellings from simple materials, including mud and sod. Today's "settlers" may devise or restore retreats from materials of equally humble provenance, or they may test their mettle in more

idiosyncratic ways. Some nomadic souls find their escape on wheels—or in homes-on-wheels, such as the venerable Airstream, which is, in essence, a modern-day evocation of the covered wagon of the Old West. No matter where these adventurous spirits alight, necessities for comfort are elemental: sky, water, fire, and food. A place to sleep might be as unpretentious as a hammock suspended between two trees, a camp cot, or a sleeping bag. To those with a New Frontier Spirit, the sky's the limit and all the world's a moon.

AIRSTREAM

A TRAVEL TRAILER

162T406

JACKSON CENTER, OHIO

Its owners take Bambi—the smallest self-contained model of Airstream built—to places too remote to have lodgings or where development is not allowed, such as in national parks. So the fact that it is entirely self-supporting—there is a gas stove, refrigerator, and hot and cold running water—is ideal.

Added to this self-sufficiency, the Bambi's compact size encourages outdoor living, as do the empty acres of desert at their disposal. But it is a very pared-down lifestyle, not unlike camping: "When you are independent of the utility grid, you become acutely aware of every drop of water and every watt of

electricity you use as well as the waste stream you produce and must deal with," say the owners. This consciousness, and the Airstream's lightweight, aircraft-type construction, inspired an "eco-restoration." Fixtures were assessed in terms of weight (for fuel-saving haulage) and ecofriendliness.

# OASIS ON WHEELS This unusual getaway vehicle was an inventive solution to a twofold problem. The owners, a husband-and-wife architect team, needed a spare room to accommodate the regular guests who visited their home in the San Francisco Bay area. They also needed an escape from the "24/7" work ethic of Silicon Valley. They own their own business, and, since it is located in their house, the only way to escape from work is to get right away.

When the owner picked up the Airstream, "it had all the aesthetic charm of a roadside men's room." Today, jt gleams-inside and out. A foldaway "porch" is an essential defense against the desert sun and wind—as is a hat.

So, the compact 16-foot trailer was acquired. Bought sight unseen over the Internet, the 1962 Airstream Bambi has adapted well to its double life. Out on the road, it is an itinerant vacation cottage, going anywhere the owners' fancy takes them. By contrast, parked in the yard at home, it makes an effective self-contained guest suite.

A mobile form of escape gives the owners a wide choice of environment. California spans 24 climate zones, and its landscape ranges from very high mountains (Mount Witney reaches 12,000 feet) to very deep canyons (Death Valley is 240 feet below sea level). But it is the desert that attracts the Airstream's owners. "The desert climate is by definition harsh, and the landscape is made even more dramatic in the winter when the sun is low in the sky. Desert winter nights can be 14 hours long, below freezing, with winds gusting up to 50 miles an hour. But Bambi tempers any weather conditions."

The trailer required extensive restoration. Nearly 30 pounds of paint was stripped off the aluminum interior, and the original heavy enameled-steel stove and sink were replaced with lightweight stainless-steel versions to help with fuel efficiency.

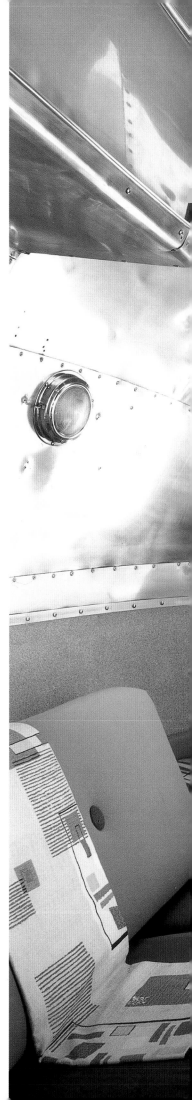

LEFT:
During the restoration, the veneered kitchen cabinets were rebuilt using aluminum, which is light and avoided the need for petrochemical finishes.

RIGHT:
Cleverly planned, the compact interior adapts from daytime to bedtime with ease—the table folds away and the sofas transform into beds.

ABOVE AND BELOW LEFT:
Retro aluminum accessories, in keeping with the vehicle's design, complete the escape fantasy—to another time as well as another place.

Low-wattage light fixtures replaced inefficient steel-and-plastic versions. The owners also replaced a sandwich of vinyl flooring, particleboard, and linoleum with two-colored stripes of a Portuguese cork that is naturally occurring and renewable, and one of the lightest floorings to be found. The stripes help to counteract the narrowness of the space. Where the original fixtures couldn't be bettered, they have been retained. The original 38-year-old propane refrigerator (no CFCs) still works, as do the propane space heater and the hot-water heater. And the tiny shower and toilet room remains unchanged—in fact, the owners say the original Italian handheld shower works better than any shower fixture in their house.

In the process of restoring the trailer's "romance of the road" character, the couple have collected aluminum artefacts—cookbook, trash can, ice chest, Ball-B-Q, and luggage—dating from the 1930s to the 1970s, largely sourced over the Internet. Retro fabrics also suit the vehicle's 1960s design and its "days gone by" atmosphere. But perhaps what most characterizes the decor are the ever-changing arrangements of leaves, sticks, colored sand, and rocks, collected by the owners on their latest escape to the desert.

The owners have spent, on average, nearly a month each year in Bambi, exploring the many possibilities of living close to nature. "It's beyond the imagination; the mix of elements is inexhaustible and unpredictable. For us, where elements clash in nature makes the best scenery, for instance an oasis in a desert, or a place where mountains meet the sea." The Airstream itself is perhaps a perfect example of this clash of extremes, forming a striking contrast between its lustrous, manmade form and the parched landscape of the desert.

LEFT:
Large windows in the kitchen make it feel as if the luxuriant yard is encroaching. Potted plants, and leaves on the glass roof, blur the boundaries between inside and out.

ABOVE:
Steps lead down from the front door to the "music room," and this, in turn, leads into the dining room and out into the yard. A ceiling fan cools the double-height space.

# MALIBU SANCTUARY

Escape, for some, means relinquishing control—letting go of hectic schedules and timetables. With its air of organic spirituality, this hillside house is part meditative space, part retreat, part jungle, part animal sanctuary, and it's still evolving. This California home is the perfect mix of dynamic natural life and utterly relaxed human existence.

Surrounded by a high fence to keep out the coyotes, the jungle-like yard is central to the house and its owner's lifestyle. Rampant vegetation seems on the point of invading everything, inside and out. The house was once owned by a nurseryman, so the yard was already full of plants when its present owner acquired it. The enveloping morning fogs provide the perfect environment for the tropical and subtropical plants that she has added. A rough concrete path leads past salvaged garden furniture to the front door, while brick paving surrounds an old fountain embellished with new mosaic.

The house in the chaparral-covered hills outside Malibu belonging to the top fashion model is still not complete, but that's how she likes it. She prefers things to be evolving rather than to reach a conclusion because, as she says, if you bring things to an end, what else can happen?

Her house is still happening. Transported from its former life of shiny brass and pink marble, it's now an easy-come, easy-go sort of place. She leads a frenetic life all over the world, but is a great animal-lover and respecter of the environment, so she was searching for somewhere that would feel at one with the natural world. With help from architect–designer Jeffrey Cayle, and in less than a year from conception to moving in, that is exactly what she has found.

Cayle retained the exterior structure of the early 1970s house, but he opened it up to the outside by adding plenty of large steel-framed windows. The spacious sunken "music room" is now the heart of the house, where all the owner's friends gather. Leading off it are the dining room and kitchen with

LEFT:
Steel-framed glass doors lead out onto a balcony from the master bedroom, helping to blur the distinction between indoors and out.

RIGHT:
The house, and its luxuriant yard, are a sanctuary for humans and animals alike. The owner's many pets include dogs, cats, and a cockatoo; and somewhere in the lush grounds, if you can find them, are the stables, home to her beloved white horse.

BELOW:
The owner is passionate about recycling, so the main staircase was made from old ironwood, charred black from the Malibu fires that raged in the region in the early 1990s. Pieces of fossilized shell, once embedded in the hillside, decorate the stair risers.

terrific views over and access to the luxuriant yard. Off the kitchen is the "womb room," a deep, dark, cozy sanctuary dominated by a fireplace carved from rock and a huge television set. A covered walkway leads to an office and a guest room. Upstairs is the meditation room, the master bedroom, and, with stunning views over the yard below, a bamboo- and plant-lined bathroom.

The yard is unforgettable. The small stream that runs through it has been adapted, so that instead of drying up for part of the year, it is constantly fed with recycled water from a pond at the bottom of the hill. Chaotic, overgrown tropical and subtropical plants flourish in the grounds—the owner can never bear to remove any plant, even if it's dead.

Meanwhile, in the cool interior, with fans whirring softly from immensely high ceilings, her many pets —even the horse—are allowed to wander at will, accompanying their mistress as she pads barefoot through the rooms. They, like her, see no difference between inside and outside. For them her unfinished sanctuary is not just an escape, it is a lair.

**TOP RIGHT:**
This quiet upstairs room proved the ideal spot for a meditation area. The floorboards were left natural, the walls painted white, and a cotton hammock was slung from wall to wall. When the owner is in residence, she uses the room for an hour every morning.

**ABOVE AND CENTER RIGHT:**
Overlooking the garden and with its walls covered with bamboo stems and living plants, the bathroom feels like an outdoor space. The hand-molded rough cement fixtures are decorated with shells.

**RIGHT:**
The owner's horse enjoys the freedom of the lush grounds.

**OPPOSITE:**
The owner is not a collector of things and had few possessions of sentimental value, so the architect took care to introduce only items that were interesting on account of their color, texture, or the story they told. The master bedroom is decorated with a relaxed mixture of objects that meet these criteria.

Her father calls Elena Colombo's house on Long Island "that shack." It is a shack—but in the nicest possible way. It has survived the ocean for a century and suits the locals' friendly lifestyle. The 31 houses here were originally built as homes for workers at a nearby brick factory, and the new owners work hard to keep them simple. Being part of a fixed group of friends, however, means there is lots of easy entertaining, too. What is so special to residents here is the feeling not just of friendship, but of shared responsibility and the enjoyment that comes from being part of a close-knit group of like minds.

# BEACH COMMUNITY

Beaches have always been about vacations, fun, children, expeditions, and parties. The beach is certainly the focal point in the life of Elena Colombo's chosen escape on the shores of eastern Long Island, only two hours' drive from Manhattan. It is part of a legally grouped commune that owns common land and has a ruling board voted in to make decisions. The jointly owned common land extends to 90 acres around the houses, so all community members can walk where they please.

OPPOSITE:
**Elena says that simple decoration suits these homes. "People here regularly go to the local antique store for finds—and there's The Barn, where people take things they no longer want. Others pick things up, so everything circulates. We're into the whole recycling vibe. There are yard sales, too, where everything is cheap and bartering is big. Nobody wants to be elegant."**

ABOVE:
**In the front porch a wire salad shaker doubles as a wall sculpture, and an oil lamp stands on a white table; flowery pillows are piled on a cheerful striped blanket.**

LEFT:
**An old round mirror above a high stool in the main kitchen area. Many of the rooms in the house retain original features, such as wooden planks or built-in closets. Their charm comes from Elena's clever use of painted walls and furniture.**

This is purely a summer community, so it has a carefree vacation atmosphere. Most cottages are decorated, just like Elena Colombo's, with casual finds from the beach and the water, and from the small local stores. She is a sculptor, and she dots her house with pieces inspired by the wind and water, created using metal, stone, wood, and bone found on or near the property.

She says that everybody does the same—a single shell on a shelf looks beautiful here. The houses are plain, with windows and wainscoting put in at the turn of the century, so simple decoration suits them.

"Many of us are friends from Manhattan, and we have gotten to know everyone and live side by side. We have beautiful sparkly dinners out on the lawns, when we all bring something to eat and set up long tables. There are kids and old people, gays and straights, blacks and whites, and everything in between. The oldest person is 85, and often the youngest has just been born. It is a true commune.

"There are spontaneous parties all the time. One friend always brings fireworks, and another has a

## WE KNOW EVERYONE. THERE ARE KIDS AND OLD PEOPLE, GAYS AND STRAIGHTS, BLACKS AND WHITES, AND EVERYTHING IN BETWEEN. THE OLDEST PERSON IS 85, AND OFTEN THE YOUNGEST HAS JUST BEEN BORN. IT IS A TRUE COMMUNE.

**ABOVE:**
Elena Colombo prides herself on using found objects to decorate the house. Some are picked up on the beach, others come from local thrift stores. The back porch shows the powerful effect that can be achieved by the artful arrangement of simple objects such as old candlesticks and tools.

**LEFT:**
The original kitchen sink is enlivened with fresh green walls and propped pictures.

**OPPOSITE:**
The main kitchen area doubles as a dining room with plain wooden chairs.

huge grill—so we just throw the fish on the grill. It's possible to fish in our inlet, and there are mussels and clams and lobster out near the sound." Also around the shores are porgies and red snapper, swordfish and tuna, and the tantalizingly named weakfish. Diamondback sea turtles can be seen, too.

Elena is enthusiastic about the positives of summer living by the water. The list begins, at least, with the smell, the colors, the opportunity to sit and watch the birds, the sailboats, the fresh fish, the sun, and the breeze. Birdwatchers in the commune can look for sea eagles, also known as ospreys, snow egrets, and the great blue heron; there are loons, belted kingfishers, and willow flycatchers, too.

Several friends keep boats here, and groups can pile in and zip to another spot across the water to swim or picnic. Two are restored mahogany runabouts that match the properties. In fact, in most aspects of life at the commune, the pressures are minimal and the pleasures great. "Whenever I come here, I just don't want to leave. I feel so lucky," Elena concludes.

**OPPOSITE:**
Like a giant galvanized bucket, the bathtub fits neatly into the tiny bathroom, which is festooned with bright beach towels.

**BELOW LEFT:**
A guest bedroom has been decorated with sea-green beaded walls, and an old mirror has been informally propped on a table between the beds.

**THIS PAGE:**
Original tongue-and-groove walls have been painted soft white, as has the iron bedstead in Elena's room. She mixes thrift-store buys and antiques in a mix of pastel shades.

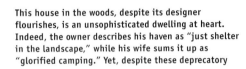

This house in the woods, despite its designer flourishes, is an unsophisticated dwelling at heart. Indeed, the owner describes his haven as "just shelter in the landscape," while his wife sums it up as "glorified camping." Yet, despite these deprecatory statements, it is an approach they have been careful to preserve. It would be all to easy to make this get-away-from-it-all spot a mirror image of their city home, with all the mod cons, but that would undermine its true purpose—to act as a quiet counterbalance to city life.

# BARN TO BE WILD

For a New York architect and his wife, this rural retreat is a place to get their hands dirty. Chopping firewood and carrying water are a welcome change from urban life. By resisting nearly all luxuries— even down to plumbed-in conveniences—they are forced to "rough it." Instead they have provided themselves with a rarer indulgence: peace and quiet and a connection with the natural world.

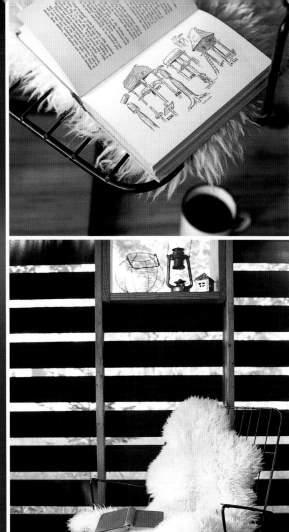

Positioned on a south-facing hillside to get morning and afternoon sun, the narrow barn is punctuated by a large picture window and ringed by translucent fiberglass slats that, with the sun beaming in, create the effect of being in a giant, airy light box united with the outside. The gaps create a visual and physical link between inside and outside.

The architect and owner of this barn on a wooded hillside in Vermont explains its appeal. "Being here is about experiencing the place itself rather than any material comforts; letting the surroundings dominate completely."

Despite the clever architectural details (and the many examples of classic mid-twentieth-century furniture), this vacation home is much more about getting back to basics than designer flourishes. There's no electricity, running water, or indoor plumbing, for instance—all water for cooking and washing is pumped by hand from the spring-fed pond. Yet for the owner, who, in his words, "works like a dog felling trees and chopping firewood" whenever he goes there, the whole experience creates the perfect counterbalance to his loft-living existence in New York City.

Having acquired the 100-acre site in Vermont several years ago, with the proviso that he wouldn't break it up, the owner unconventionally set about "inhabiting" the landscape by first creating a pond, then a meadow, and then a hot tub, before finally starting on the barn or "hovel" as he calls it, many weekend work parties later. "Putting it simply, it's just a shelter in the landscape. For me the kick comes from editing that landscape, opening vistas, making

the surroundings more airy. This is the way it would have been in the 1800s when this was a hillside farm with more meadow than trees, rather than the other way around as it was when we bought the place."

With a high peaked roof of corrugated metal, and 63 feet long by only 10 feet wide, the building draws its inspiration from indigenous agricultural buildings, like the covered bridges and tobacco-drying barns for which the region is famous. However, for its ventilation, a "dog-trot" or open passageway that bisects the building, the architect-owner looked to the South. Thanks to this, even in the height of summer a cool breeze steals through the space. It's full of light, too. The slatted sides of the house appear open to the elements, but are actually interleaved with translucent fiberglass, which allows light in and out—to pretty effect at night—while being watertight and bugproof. Great thought has gone into the placement of windows for the best light, views, and cooling breezes. The high-level window—matched by one at the opposite end of the barn—provides effective through-ventilation. And since the property isn't overlooked, there is no need for window treatments beyond screens.

Jutting out into the valley on concrete pillars, 1,400 feet above sea level, the house was designed

MAIN PICTURE:
**The upright stairs—in true settler fashion—lead to a space-saving sleeping platform in the eaves, shown opposite below right.**

ABOVE AND OPPOSITE ABOVE RIGHT:
**This home proves that space is a relative concept. Even large rooms can feel cramped if they are badly lit or stuffed with excess furniture and possessions. By contrast, the barn is decorated in space-enhancing, airy colors—white and the palest greens, with blue touches—and has clever storage features such as the drawers under the window seat, above.**

LEFT:
**Eating outside— breakfast, lunch, and dinner—is one of the great pleasures of life. Daily groceries are bought from a local organic farm.**

OPPOSITE AND BELOW:
**The property was acquired on the understanding that it would be kept intact. The owner has added only natural features such as the pond.**

to take in the south-facing views of the surrounding mountains and the Connecticut River valley. "We get the best views and the best weather here. Although for me there's no such thing as unpleasant weather: listening to the rain falling, walking through the snow, and heating the place with wood in the winter are all pleasurable aspects of being here—ways to connect back with the rituals of life—just as are physically working hard, carrying water, and chopping wood. My time here becomes a sort of meditation through work." And yet there is fun, too, derived from the immediacy of nature and the elements: diving in the pond in summer; skating on it in winter; soaking in the hot tub outdoors; watching the visiting wildlife—deer, bears, wild ducks and turkeys, and the occasional moose—pass by; and shopping for berries, bread, flowers, and cheese from the organic farm stand miles back along the dirt track. Of course, the simplest pleasures are often the most rewarding. The wood-fired hot tub was installed even before the barn, and makes a rudimentary yet sensual way to enjoy bathing out of doors, all year round — whatever the weather. All that is needed is water, wood for burning, privacy, and a bewitching aspect.

While his ability to rough it might be unusual, the owner's need for the haven as a balance to— but not a substitution for—his other, urban life is not. Asked could he imagine living here all year round, he answered succinctly, "Yes, but no," before expanding, "I'm very comfortable in the country, doing what I do there, but I enjoy it more when it is held in contrast to the city side of my life. I like the grit and push of New York, but I also like the absolute quiet of Vermont."

## THERE'S NO SUCH THING AS UNPLEASANT WEATHER: LISTENING TO THE RAIN FALLING AND WALKING THROUGH THE SNOW ARE PLEASURABLE ASPECTS OF BEING HERE.

OPPOSITE:
The front porch illustrates how Barbara honors the legacy of the house. The screen door is the spindle-accented type often found in country houses at the turn of the century. Barbara trucked the blue shutters all the way from her former house in New Jersey—and was pleased to find they fit perfectly.

ABOVE LEFT:
The front door into the house is enlivened with moldings that lend the effect of raised paneling. A collection of walking sticks fills an Adirondack-style basket made locally; these, worn on the back, were used as pack baskets. The mahogany banister remains essentially as is, even with some spindles replaced.

ABOVE RIGHT:
In the living room, a shapely Gustavian clock hints at the Swedish design influences that inform the decorating scheme. Barbara purchased all the sisal rugs scattered throughout the house from the old Conran's store in Manhattan. Sackcloth slung over the back of a chair bears its original stamp.

# THIS OLD HOUSE
A permanent move to the country can be triggered by one or more of any number of circumstances—a yearning for the simple life, a job, retirement. Whatever the motive, a sense of place figures in the decision of where to put down roots. For Barbara Davis, an antique dealer and interior designer, making the switch from suburban New Jersey, and its easy proximity to Manhattan, to upstate New York was the fulfillment of a dream. She longed to live in—and care for —an old house. The one she found was everything she wished for, and more.

OPPOSITE:
The hall exemplifies Barbara's laissez-faire attitude to the house. The plaster behind the old wallboard was stable enough to mount a few treasured items, including a length of rope-accented trim. Twig "hooks" hold a pair of wooden children's snowshoes from Sweden, a trug-style basket, a French "filet," or string bag, and other items. The table is a "country hepplewhite."

Where Barbara landed, after an extensive search all over New York State, was the rangy, rolling farmland near Cooperstown, a thriving summer colony that is home to the Glimmerglass Opera and Baseball Hall of Fame. The rest of the year, the town is a quiet haven for all who make it their full-time home. For Barbara, the town—and the area—presented the best of two worlds: a place to rebuild her interior design business, and a place to bring up her four children, who range in age from 16 to three.

Her primary goal was to find a house in its "original condition," as she says, not one that had been tampered with or "improved" beyond recognition. Like many American homesteads, the dwelling place she settled on had expanded over the years from a simple one-and-a-half story Colonial to a house over twice the size; the last major addition, built in the 1820s, gobbled up an old kitchen and ended up being larger than the original section of the house—a not uncommon phenomenon in the Northeast. What appealed to Barbara most, though, was the fact that no one had touched the house in over 50 years. Nor had anyone tilled its 20 acres; in fact, the hill right behind the house is—inch by inch—being reclaimed by woods.

Where most people might have perceived the house as dissolving into a state of benign neglect, Barbara

ABOVE AND ABOVE LEFT:
The kitchen assembles necessities, including a 1940s range (and fridge), a stainless-steel sink and cabinet, and a worktable, with a rich mix of dishes and other sundries. Barbara made the stacking storage units; doors are old windows. The partitioned piece over the stove came from a post office and was used for sorting mail. The dyed panels on the wall set off Barbara's collections.
RIGHT:
Off the kitchen is the sunroom she uses as a potting shed.

OPPOSITE:
Barbara constructed the pine screen behind the living-room sofa; she likes the way its zigzag profile breaks up the boxiness of the room. She also built the cupboard—around a pair of shutters revitalized as doors.

ABOVE AND RIGHT:
The stair landing is a bright spot to curl up or do projects. The recamier-style daybed wears under-upholstery made of striped hessian; Barbara stuffed the pillows with straw. The straw matting on the wall was rolled up in the attic. When she discovered it would fit between the eave and the window, Barbara hung it behind the daybed. The writing desk may be Scandinavian.

LEFT:
A former wallpaper-hanger's table stands in the corner of Barbara's office. She replaced the top with a sheet of plexiglass, which she uses to display her antique, hand-dyed fabrics.

ABOVE RIGHT:
The generous width of the rope chair in Barbara's baby's room indicates that it was probably cut down from a bed. The two fishing creels in the room are joined by a wire basket used to store a day's catch under water until time came to clean it.

LEFT:
The master bedroom opens from the landing. The French iron bedstead stands against a wall Barbara painted a shade of green she mixed herself; she also made the stencil, adapting it from a Swedish motif. Pillows are damask.

**BECAUSE WINTERS ARE DARK, BARBARA WANTED TO LIGHTEN UP EVERY ROOM AS MUCH AS POSSIBLE; THE TRADITIONAL SWEDISH PALETTE OF SKY BLUE, GRAY-GREEN, AND WHITE FIT THE BILL.**

ABOVE:
In her daughter's room, the bed is French. Barbara's grandfather made the baby-blue dollhouse when Barbara was a little girl. The rag mat by the bed is Amish.

saw integrity and charm. Therefore, interventions she has imposed upon the house have been gradual and minor—only enough to effect what she carefully terms an "un-restoration." Unsightly, intrusive elements, such as a 1940s dropped ceiling, and rotting, half-century-old wallboard that protruded beyond the moldings, had to go, but rough plaster that covered the walls turned out to be fairly stable, so, rather than paint them, Barbara decided to leave them be. In the end, she did paint the master bedroom, but only to give herself a colorful background she could stencil with a design she adapted from one used in a museum in Sweden.

Swedish design inspired the color palette, too. Because winters are dark, with the sun setting as early as 4:30 P.M., Barbara wanted to lighten up every room as much as possible; the traditional Swedish palette of sky blue, gray-green, and white fit the bill. Once she'd settled on her color scheme, Barbara dyed many of the antique, natural-fiber textiles used throughout the house in varying shades of blue. She also stripped all the hardwood floors of a brittle layer of polyurethane, leaving some to show off the warm wood, and painting others white. To gently "antique" the white floors, she brushed on a watery glaze in a soft, dove-gray hue.

Furnishings throughout the house are also in the condition in which Barbara found them. In her old antiquing days, she had traveled widely throughout New England, and many of her favorite finds remained with her until she could secure a suitable background to show them off. She found it here.

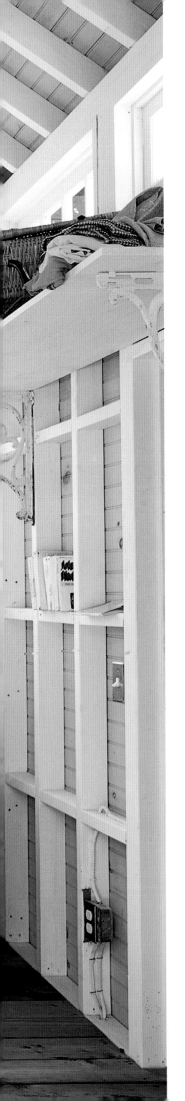

LEFT:
One sunroom is like a beach cabana, with its framing exposed to reveal tongue-and-groove siding painted the slate blue of a mist-veiled sky. An awning-striped spread drapes over the daybed; pillows are covered in cotton ticking.

ABOVE:
Porches are inviting outdoor rooms. On one, a green bench swings on chains.

ABOVE RIGHT:
On another, a roll-around camp bed is swagged with mosquito netting.

RIGHT:
Just beyond it, an outdoor shower is protected by a curtain made of sailcloth.

# EAST END MAGIC

The eastern end of New York's Long Island divides—like a tailfin—into the so-called North and South Forks. For decades, farmers in these parts grew potatoes. Now many fields are vineyards—or host to vacation getaways for the rich and famous. Here and there, though, pockets of calm persist; like the unpretentious house featured here, they offer welcome respite.

**ABOVE AND LEFT:**
Places to relax and congregate occur throughout the house; furniture is arranged in companionable circular groups, which naturally draw people closer together. Floors slicked with linen-white marine deck paint unite all rooms.

**OPPOSITE:**
The entrance hall is separated from the adjoining parlor by a pair of room-high salvaged doors whose glass panes are crusted and scoured by age. The front-door surround also shows signs of decay.

The ocean's siren call beckons many who call the city home. Restive from work, or simply hungry for an antidote to high-rises and concrete, hordes of urbanites in cities as diverse as San Francisco, Chicago, Washington, D.C.—and New York —stream forth every weekend to places as far from the madding crowd as they can manage—within a sensible driving distance. For Manhattanites, "sensible" can mean two to three hours spent behind the wheel, depending upon traffic; despite the distance and the hassle of getting there, a great number gravitate to Long Island's East End.

The main attraction for most is the beaches, which are among the most luxuriant along the eastern seaboard. Sparkling white and ruffled by dune grass, Long Island's beaches—especially those that border the Atlantic Ocean (as opposed to those along the gentle, Long Island Sound that washes the North Fork)—are particularly roomy and hospitable.

For years, East End villages were simple farming and fishing communities composed of humble, unassuming shingle-sided cottages linked by long stretches of low-lying bayberry, scrub pine, and

potato fields. Only Sag Harbor—which, along with
Nantucket, was a thriving center for a once-booming
whaling industry—boasted mansions worthy of note.

It was only a matter of time, though, before the
area was discovered by New Yorkers. Initially, it was
the artists who came, drawn by a special, ineffable
quality of light, and by a simple lifestyle. Today, the
"season" between Memorial Day and Labor Day
witnesses an explosion of day-trippers, weekenders,
and summer residents, all yearning for escape.

For this reason, finding a house that feels cut off
from the world is an almost unimaginable feat. But
that is just what the family whose house is featured
here pulled off. Surrounded by mature trees, it is an
oasis, one that refreshes them every time they visit.

It is a magical place, at once snug and cozy, yet
airy and full of light. Much of the magic comes from
the way the interiors of the house blend with the
out-of-doors. Wherever possible, walls are opened
up with banks of windows, which allow the sun to
penetrate even the darkest corners at all times of
day. When opened, they allow for cross-ventilation,
a requisite for the humid dog days of summer.
Porches and decks offer myriad opportunities for
being outside; one, for example, doubles as a guest
room, while another, shared with the master suite,
plays host to an outdoor shower.

The architectural vernacular on the porches and in the
sunrooms is that of the beach: exposed framing and
rafters; a weathered shutter; scrubbed, but otherwise
unfinished floorboards or decking. By contrast,
decorative embellishments in many rooms, including
delicate crystal chandeliers, chintz slipcovers and
draperies, and vintage lace-trimmed bedclothes, hint
at a romantic and sophisticated sense of the urbane.
The palette is pale, to magnify the light, and, because
this is primarily a summer place, floors are, for the most
part, left bare—a boon for sweeping up after sandy feet.

MAIN PICTURE:
In a beadboard-
wrapped sunroom, a
wide ledge accented
with Carpenter-Gothic
trim is cantilevered
from beneath the
windows to provide
ample stretch-out
space for two—even
for guests who decide
to stay the night. A
tempting miscellany
of pillows, including
oversized European
squares, plump out to
become backrests
along the windowsills.
The old-fashioned
wooden Venetian
blinds counteract the
glare of the sun.

FAR RIGHT ABOVE:
A white iron bedstead
just barely slides in
under the tall eave of
an attic bedroom. An

extra-long lace panel
is knotted around a
hook at the peak of
the ceiling, then
drapes seductively
along the top of the
window, tethered there
by a narrow rod.

FAR RIGHT BELOW:
The master bedroom
contains a vintage-
style soaking tub,
which is secreted from
view behind a folding
screen. Behind the bed
stands another, carved
Asian screen. Reclining
in the tub is a doubly
sensual experience, as
the bather may gaze
through lace-draped
French doors to a deck
and trees beyond. The
corner fireplace and
wing chair are cozy
comforts come fall
and winter.

# CONTEMPORARY
## INSPIRATION

E very era has its avant-garde, usually artists and other creative souls seeking to escape from the confines of the tried-and-true. In architecture and design, the term cutting-edge applies not only —as expected—to urban structures, but also to buildings in rural, and, in some cases, remote places. Here, centuries collide and coalesce in distinctive dwelling places that flex their muscles in novel and exciting ways. Here, the tension between a traditional need for comfort and an iconoclastic desire to surprise results in houses as unique as their owners. These are hideaways that are singular in every sense of the word. Materials run the gamut from fir and pine to plastic and polymers, from adobe and brick to glass and metallic alloys. The challenges of combining and juxtaposing conventional and unexpected materials are magnified in the wild, of course, but savvy architects and designers meet them head-on, creating habitats for living that function well and are a pleasure to be in. The hallmarks of these designs are a scrupulous attention to

detail and exquisite craftsmanship. The dialogue between site and structure is terse and to the point: It's a virile, Popeye the Sailor Man "I Yam what I Yam" attitude that pervades these places. Strong and muscular, the houses dare to stand out from the norm, and from their neighbors—if any. They are clearly contemporary in look, mood, and feel.

OPPOSITE:
From a distance, the Idaho house appears to hunker down in a landscape as texturally rough as pumice stone; upon closer inspection, though, it straddles a streambed lush with sagebrush, willow, and aspen.

ABOVE LEFT:
Architect Jim Ruscitto designed the flat-roofed house to follow a cruciform plan; logs jut out beyond exterior walls to create baffles for courtyards and decks.

TOP RIGHT AND ABOVE RIGHT:
Windows frame specific vignettes of the view. Stucco is pigmented to give the appearance of adobe. The sun-bleached skull of a steer hangs over the entry.

# SCULPTURAL HOMESTEAD

America is a nation of microclimates. In some regions of the country, the weather—and the vegetation—can change within a mere mile. One such juxtaposition occurs in central Idaho where the vast Midwestern basin desert meets the Western Rockies. At this convergence was the spot the original owners of this house fell in love with as the environment for their new home. This is sagebrush country; a mile north, forestlands begin. It is a place blessed by the gifts of Nature.

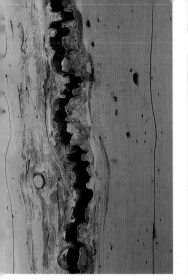

ABOVE:
**Spruce-log walls have smaller knots than Douglas-fir columns.**

TOP LEFT AND CENTER:
**"Feature logs"—some 3½ feet thick—exhibit idiosyncrasies such as this slash burned into the wood by lightning. A birch-bark lamp is a natural accent.**

LEFT:
**The sculptural chimneypiece rises against a log partition that was "feathered" along its edge.**

For the original owners of the house, the site they selected—a five-acre lot in a subdivision near the ski resort where they ran an art gallery—presented an unexpected bonus: unlike many housing plots in this part of the country, it is essentially a bog webbed by streams, an ecosystem the husband, a wildflower biologist, couldn't resist. But, a bog is not without its drawbacks. For one thing, how do you build on unstable ground? Local architect Jim Ruscitto met the challenge head on: He erected the residence on 135 pilings driven deep into the soggy earth; the house, and its companion master suite, ford the streambeds percolating through the bog on these pilings. A glass bridge connects the two.

THIS PAGE:
The 22-foot-high living room is highlighted by a serpentine balcony, which bellies into the space. Windows at the roofline make the roof appear to be "resting on a ribbon of light." Windows and floor function as a passive-solar system; shale stores and radiates the sun's warmth, even on cloudy days. Hefty furniture complements the room's size.

OPPOSITE:
**The kitchen fits snugly under the balcony. Log ends viewed outside the balcony-high window next to the kitchen mirror those that rise in a syncopated rhythm along the edge of an interior partition. The ladder leaning against the partition is draped with a pair of Navajo blankets; the basket behind them is Cherokee.**

RIGHT:
**The "sun-pocket" off the kitchen doubles as a breakfast room. Facing southeast, it pulls in the sun's rays until noon each day.**

The pilings provide support for a mix of materials —log, shale, glass, and stucco that's saturated with pigment the color of Southwestern adobe—that coalesce to form a homestead that speaks its own unique vernacular. Logs and adobe root the house to an American past while glass (and Sheetrock) place it firmly in modern times. To accomplish this, the architect first erected four massive log walls, which intersect to form a cross. The quadrants created in the spaces between the arms of the cross are built in the time-honored post-and-beam manner; these became the armature for a conventional wall system that would support wide expanses of glass.

The south-facing quadrants of the house take advantage of the full force of the winter sun; here the sheets of glass pull in the low sun's rays so they fall on a floor covered entirely in shale. Together with a concrete subfloor, the stone retains the warmth built up during the day; the stone releases heat as twilight descends. During the summer, when the sun is high, the precise placement of the windows inhibits rays from penetrating the inner reaches of the house.

ABOVE RIGHT:
**Doorways leading off the balcony into the guest rooms are built in the standard log-home manner, with exposed log-ends butting the jambs.**

RIGHT:
**The sinuous, winding stair, like the balcony, stands out from the stark, rectilinear walls that frame the windows.**

BELOW:
**One column ends in a seat on the balcony.**

Windows turn views into pictures. Ruscitto paced the site to ascertain how best to create vignettes; thus, a tall, vertical window zeroes in on one specific nearby peak, while clerestories at the roofline outline the panoramic silhouette visible from the site.

The log walls—and a number of interior partitions—are stacked in the Swedish coping style, without chinking. As logs settle, they hug each other ever more tightly. At times they even creak, and split, emitting cracks as sharp as thunder. All of the wood came from standing-dead trees, including several gigantic Douglas-fir logs used as columns to punctuate the Great Room's double-story open space.

The columns, three feet in diameter, support an undulating balcony that overlooks the room; an equally sculptural winding stair leads to guest rooms. The sculptural elements—including a modulated chimneypiece that alludes to Southwestern kiva-style adobe fireplaces—were designed, Ruscitto says, to "contradict" the rustic logs, as well as the strict, flat white walls that enclose the windows.

A few years ago, the house was sold. The current owners fell so in love with the place they decided to live here full time. Inspired by the architecture, they treat the house as much as a piece of sculpture as the former owners did. So, the legacy of art and nature continues. It's the best of both worlds.

## AS LOGS SETTLE, THEY HUG EACH OTHER MORE TIGHTLY. THEY CREAK, AND SPLIT, EMITTING CRACKS AS SHARP AS THUNDER.

OPPOSITE:
A corner of the master bathroom shows how tightly logs interlock in the chink-free Swedish coping style. Spikes below the bottle-cap cross were recovered from the railroad spur that once served this part of Idaho.

ABOVE LEFT:
The master bedroom occupies its own discrete "pod" that was constructed 25 feet —and across a narrow creek— from the main house; it connects to the house via a glass bridge.

ABOVE RIGHT:
Stacking logs poses a problem: how to align two walls? Sometimes bottom-most logs—as here —must be sliced in half, or trimmed.

RIGHT:
A contemporary hickory chair looks old.

ABOVE:
The house is so well integrated with the landscape that its overall scale is hard to grasp. From some approaches, the building seems to merge with its thickly wooded setting, while from other directions, it has a solid, even intimidating presence.

OPPOSITE:
Concrete planes and wooden decks shape external rooms that extend beyond the living areas into the landscape. Wood-framed glass walls lend lightness and transparency to the interior, making a connection with the natural surroundings in all their wild magnificence. A right-angled concrete wall reaches out beyond the the western end of the house, but its austerity is tempered and softened by planting. The concrete extends the house into the landscape, forging a link between ground and architecture, and helps to anchor the house to the land.

# APPALACHIAN BALANCING ACT
The Mountain House was designed for a couple with varied interests—he is a journalist and collector of regional art; she is a gardener and landscape designer. In search of aesthetic equilibrium for their weekend retreat (and future retirement home), they commissioned a building that accommodates their differences by finding common ground. The outcome brings contrasting elements together: inside and out, light and shade, intimacy and openness. Here in this light-filled modern home, set in ancient woods, the transition from city to countryside is complete.

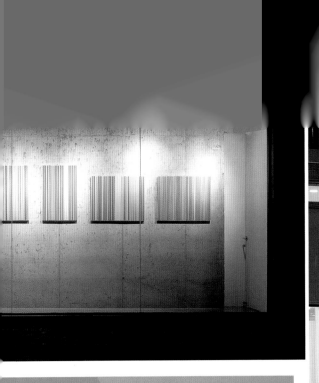

ABOVE AND TOP
CENTER:
The courtyard is paved
with local stone. The
interior wall, on view
to visitors, offers
plenty of space for
hanging pictures.

TOP LEFT:
Steps lead up to the
raised terrace around
the living space. Sheer
glass separates
indoors and out.

LEFT AND FAR LEFT:
The rustic yet elegant
character of the living
room is reinforced by
polished wood floors.
Plywood chairs based
on a classic design by
Charles and Ray Eames
cast bulbous shadows
on the floor.

Set in the foothills of the Appalachian Mountains less than a mile from Georgia's border with North Carolina, this secluded site is thickly wooded and surrounded by rolling mountains. A small stream runs across the property's southern edge, supplying power for an old grist mill and water for horses in a neighbor's pasture. Drawn by the landscape, light, and tranquility, a group of artists has established a colony nearby.

The owners asked their architects, Mack Scogin Merrill Elam, for just two things: wall space for their artworks and extensive views of the landscape. They got a long, low house that hugs the ground, in contrast to the slender birches and poplars around it. As part of the balancing act that characterizes this home, the architects opened up the house along much of the southern side, to give vistas to the creek and pasture, and a long porch connects the house to outdoors. The northern side is more closed off, providing wall space to display the owners' art.

**ABOVE AND BELOW, FAR LEFT:**
The spacious living room is linked to the terrace decks by sliding doors. The room is suffused with a delicate, shimmering light. Clerestory windows give the impression that the roof is floating overhead.

**ABOVE LEFT:**
Harmony between house and setting is evident in the play of reflections on glass.

**RIGHT:**
Strips of glass at the top and bottom of walls break up their mass.

**LEFT:**
The placing of the windows forms abstract geometric patterns.

ABOVE:
The guest house is a comfortable, self-contained refuge with its own outdoor porch overlooking one of the site's two ponds.

LEFT AND FAR LEFT, ABOVE AND BELOW:
The kitchen is linked to the bedroom and entrance hall by a long corridor, which provides space for displaying the owners' art collection. Bare concrete walls act as a neutral backdrop for vivid paintings. The main bedroom has low windows incised into the walls.

The interiors are suffused with shimmering light, both from the sun and the moon. The owners love the way the light animates the whole house. They also like the fact that the screened porch acts as a second living room, playing country cousin to the more urban indoor one on the other side. Equipped with a built-in concrete bench, a large grill, and underfloor heating, the porch can be used all year round for entertaining. These expansive spaces can accommodate a crowd, yet hideaways are scattered through the house, such as the inglenook behind the living-room fireplace, or the little bay window on the master bathroom that opens out on a private court enclosed by hemlocks. Once again, this welcoming yet intimate home is perfectly in balance.

**ABOVE:**
The lack of cupboard doors in the kitchen reflects the theme of "exposure" in this reclaimed home. This informality softens the effect of the steel.

**LEFT:**
The new open-framed mezzanine structure, made of exposed wooden beams and supported on diagonal braced columns, was put together on site. It separates the private areas on the upper level from the more public areas beneath.

## CANALSIDE REVIVAL

There is a brutal attractiveness—a no-nonsense symmetry and order—about old industrial buildings. Designed to be workplaces, they were envisaged as useful rather than beautiful, although some late-nineteenth century tycoons embellished the exteriors of their buildings with elaborate decoration or examples of their craft or trade. The restoration of a small brick factory in New Jersey transformed a canalside industrial building into a home for an owner who had long admired it. Its history is proudly on show—exposed brickwork, metal truss ceiling, and bare areas of concrete floor—but its simple utility recalls the unadorned rural homes of centuries past.

ABOVE:
Part of the factory has been left as it was to provide a work studio: a large open space with a concrete floor, brick walls, open metal truss ceiling, and steel pivot windows.

RIGHT:
The main living–dining area, showing the mezzanine support.

The Atlantic Terra Cotta Company brickworks was built on the banks of the Delaware and Raritan Canal, New Jersey, at the end of the nineteenth century, but failed to prosper throughout the whole of the twentieth. Writer and curator Alastair Gordon lived in the neighborhood as a teenager and used to walk in the grounds of the dilapidated building. For years, he nursed an ambition to revive the brickworks, but as his home rather than a business. In the early Nineties Gordon and his partner, fashion designer Barbara de Vries, visited the area and found that the property was still empty. They negotiated a long-term lease and, with the help of architects Henry Smith-Miller and Laurie Hawkinson, set about adapting the building into a habitable space.

The interior of the building is large—approximately 3,000 square feet—and double the height of an ordinary living space. To break up the vastness and create a second level, a substantial 13-foot-high platform, with slightly splayed supporting legs, was constructed. The lumber used for the platform is a natural, pale wood joined and supported by cast-aluminum saddles and corner brackets.

**ABOVE:**
The open staircase to the upper floor.

**LEFT:**
The dining area is flooded with light from the large windows, whose original sandblasted panes were replaced with clear glass. The double-height plastic panels used to conceal the work studio, behind the dining area, also allow light to circulate.

**ABOVE, TOP, AND LEFT:** Rooms on the upper floor are unadorned, while the building's exposed rafters enhance the "old factory" aesthetic of this home. The dividing doors run on tracks set in the mezzanine structure. White-coated insulation material has been strapped to the roof to reduce noise and retain warmth.

These materials are in keeping with the age and utilitarian roots of the building as well as the earthy redness of its clay-brick exterior. The platform was also designed to appear to be temporary and light, taking up most but not all of the width of the room, as opposed to a solid structure that would have been anchored to the walls. The edges of the platform are finished with waist-high railings infilled with rigid transparent panels that provide a definitive and secure edge, but do not make it feel restricted or hemmed in. The transparent panels also allow a plentiful supply of daylight to the upper rooms.

On the upper level are the master bedroom, a bathroom, a second living room, and de Vries's spacious study and work space. The large bathroom is equipped with a vintage rolltop bathtub, deep double basins, and a huge mirror—large-scale furnishings work well in this oversized building.

Downstairs are a library, another sitting area, and a dining area running alongside a galley kitchen with units built in under galvanized metal surfaces.

## GORDON USED TO WALK IN THE GROUNDS OF THE DILAPIDATED BUILDING. FOR YEARS, HE NURSED AN AMBITION TO REVIVE THE BRICKWORKS.

These living, entertaining, and cooking spaces are all contained under the platform, leaving the unfurnished perimeter of the ground floor to act as a corridor between the inner living area and the outer walls. The edges of the platform were specially designed to finish a yard or two in front of the 10-feet-high windows so the natural light and views were uninterrupted. Original sandblasted windowpanes were replaced with clear glass, again to enhance the flow of light and access to views.

A new concrete floor was laid on the ground floor, and softer, warmer birch plywood flooring was used upstairs and in Gordon's office. The roof was insulated, and the insulation was covered with a white membrane held in place by narrow strips of wood. The solid walls—such as those between the bedroom and landing/second living room and the wall behind the headboard—were painted white, again to reflect light, but also to reinforce the simple, uncluttered look of the place. Sliding translucent plastic panels were put at the end of the ground-floor living space to close off Gordon's work area beyond. The plastic allows light to filter through from the windows in the work area, but provides insulation that keeps the heat localized when the living area is in use. The sliding walls also obscure the view of the space beyond, making it feel cozier and more intimate at the living-room end of the building, especially at night.

ABOVE:
Fixtures in the factory have an unfinished look that suits the setting. Mechanical, electrical, and air-conditioning systems are all exposed to view.

RIGHT:
The mezzanine level was installed to add more living space and reduce height. It is freestanding, so the barnlike feeling of open space is retained.

The rambling form of this Maine home weaves and dodges through the forest like an informal camp, becoming part of the landscape. Glass opens up the house to spectacular views and light, emphasizing the natural connection.

ABOVE:
In response to the sloping terrain, parts of the building are supported on slim columns that emulate the surrounding tree trunks while they minimize disturbance to the site.

LEFT:
A ramp resembling a drawbridge leads up to the main entrance, providing a ceremonial approach.

OPPOSITE MAIN PICTURE:
The simple beauty of the house is complemented with a few pieces of classic modern furniture and understated heirlooms.

FAR LEFT, TOP TO BOTTOM:
The intimate, clustered form of the house brings nature into close contact with the interior. Framed views of the landscape constantly surprise and delight. The opening in the wall enclosing the covered porch (center) brings nature in by allowing snow, rain, and light to enter the house.

This house's owner, a painter and interior designer, moved from Venice Beach in Los Angeles to Maine, on the extreme reaches of the East Coast, after the earthquake of 1994. She bought a plot in White Mountains National Park, overlooking a lake, where she commissioned architects Mack Scogin Merrill Elam to create a house with ample space for living, painting, and entertaining that would satisfy her desire to be close to nature.

The property, which covers just over 2½ acres, yields an intimate view across the lake to Lord's Hill, the easternmost boundary of the national park. The hill comforts with summer and spring greenery, dazzles with autumn colors, and shimmers and glistens in winter snow and ice. The architects were careful to disturb the site's extraordinarily fragile and beautiful ecosystem, with its delicate carpet of mossy plants, as little as possible. The northern side of the plot slopes up to a street; the south, down to the lake. A low concrete curb was used to divide the site into two parts, making a clear distinction between the man- and nature-oriented precincts.

South of the curb, the architects maximized views by lifting the house into the trees on slender wood and steel columns. A switchback path crosses under the house, working its way toward the lake edge. Cement-board panels are bolted to the house's

It is still part of the American dream to own a house on its own defined plot of land. Such a home serves as a moated castle and refuge, a place in which to withdraw from the world. This artist's dwelling reflects her needs and tastes, and represents a truly personal escape. The architects observed that it could not have been built for anyone else.

**ABOVE AND RIGHT:**
Like a modern version of a treehouse, the living room is a glazed aerie hovering above the forest. Angular and dramatic, it forms the prow of the house, a place of light, warmth, and shelter. At night (see pages 196–7), it glows like a welcoming beacon. A modern hearth forms the focus of the living space, but instead of being solid and massive, it is set in a glazed wall, framed by trees, recreating the idea of a campfire in a forest.

**BELOW RIGHT:**
The way upstairs is marked by glimpses of the forest through columns of glass.

**OPPOSITE LEFT:**
The main staircase winds up two storys, around a glazed open space. This exposure to the elements brings daylight into the deep recesses of the house.

**OPPOSITE MAIN PICTURE:**
A cubic tower hovers over and marks the house's threshold, its crisp geometry making a strong contrast with the lushness and wildness of nature.

## THE HOUSE BREATHES IN ITS SITE—FRAMING, FOCUSING, ENCLOSING, AND CELEBRATING IT. INTERIORS ARE PLANNED TO REVEAL A VIEW, FILTER LIGHT, OR CREATE A POETIC PAUSE, ALL OF WHICH ENRICH THE EXPERIENCE OF LIVING IN IT.

exterior walls and raised underbelly; the variegated light gray siding responds to the effects of rain, snow, and sun with subtle patterns.

Nature is brought indoors, too. The main staircase, lined with books, winds up two storys around a mysterious glazed open space that brings light right into the house. Rainwater replenishes a pool in its center, while reflections of books and sky play off the water, glass, and bookshelves. The stair leads to a set of small rooms that look and feel like elevated garden pavilions floating among the branches.

This glass aerie marks a return to the forest and the studio for an artist too long removed from both; her new home includes a drawing studio and a detached painting studio. The house breathes in its site—framing, focusing, enclosing, and celebrating it, so the rooms are always in communication with each other. Interiors are carefully planned to reveal a view, filter light, or create a poetic pause, all of which enrich the experience of living in it.

ABOVE:
Bought as a one-bedroom, one-bathroom shack with a gallery, the property originally captivated the owners with its sense of openness and airiness. Intriguingly, rumor had it that the original structure was built from a kit in 1972 by a Pan Am pilot.

RIGHT:
The bay is less than a minute's walk away from the property, and it is possible to canoe literally from the doorstep via the creek that runs by the house. The owner says, "We're constantly on or by the water, swimming or plopping our kayaks into the creek.

The water is a constant, reassuring presence." Even the ferry ride to get here is relaxing: "Once you're on the boat you feel totally remote and cut off from things. The minute I'm on the water I feel like I'm on vacation—it acts like a moat, isolating us from our hectic lives."

# BACK TO NATURE IN STYLE
This vacation home proves that a sense of freedom, and a physical escape, need not be far away, or involve a self-conscious change of style. It's not that far from the city—but you need to cross the water to get there. And the owners have brought their love of pure colors and modern design with them. Outdoors, there's a deserted beach to swim from and a creek to kayak on. Indoors, an almost pure white interior brings calm contentment as a respite from a busy life.

OPPOSITE AND BELOW:
**Cedar decking rings the house, forming a gentle link between the pristine interior and the deer-inhabited woods beyond.**

RIGHT:
**Earthy tones—terra cotta, tan, and dark brown—in a guest bedroom. They make a contrast to the bright white used in much of the house.**

RIGHT:
**The architects who designed the house's extension are now regular visitors. For them, it is a very grounded, down-to-earth house; a place guests immediately feel at home. The owner describes the atmosphere as "happy and childlike."**

For many people, spending time in a vacation home is all the more satisfying because it provides a complete contrast to the location, and occupation, in which they spend most of their days. Just as a sauna and plunge pool wouldn't be as refreshingly invigorating or intensely soothing without the other for contrast, an escape cannot be such without a contrasting existence to come from.

A jet-setting New York ceramicist, the owner of this island retreat, was seeking just such a contrast: "A mellow, happy getaway; a place for my partner to write, me to make pottery, and our Norfolk terrier—Liberace—to gambol; somewhere quite different from the insanity of New York." He found an area only a short ferry crossing from Long Island, and loves the sense of transition from real life to vacation time this journey gives. "By the time we arrive on the island, we are effectively misanthropic shut-ins—to the extent that we become almost feral, barely bothering to wash or get dressed! We cook, chill, frolic, and take dips on the deserted beach and that's about it."

The house had just one bedroom, so after considering geodesic domes and airstream trailers to provide the extra sleeping space they needed for guests, the owners finally commissioned architects to create an extension that fitted with and balanced the existing asymmetrical house. The new part of the house was designed to maintain the handmade,

A wood stove in the living room creates a dramatic focal point and provides the only source of heat. The owners created the quirky fireplace from found stones and pebbles. Simple, natural materials like plywood and stone have been given a low-key, subtle textural role by the uniform paint scheme. The blanket covering of white gloss paint hides a multitude of sins, bringing together a hodgepodge of disparate materials and styles to create a clean and airy atmosphere that is unthreateningly modern.

**LEFT AND RIGHT:**
Classic white paint provides a blank canvas against which to display more homey, personal elements, like the owner's own pottery and a bedspread featuring a giant snail shell which he made specially for the house. It's a look he describes as "modern rustic." The architects designed the horizontal windows in the master bedroom extension to give privacy while allowing an eye-level panorama of the enveloping leaves and branches; a sort of living wallpaper border.

**BELOW RIGHT:**
Blue and white is a classic combination for a lake- or seaside escape; think of sky, clouds and the white spray on energetic waves. Blue is used as an accent color to great effect against the white ground of much of this home. Even this glass in the living room fireplace looks striking.

## WE'RE CONSTANTLY ON OR BY THE WATER, SWIMMING OR PLOPPING OUR KAYAKS INTO THE CREEK. IT IS A CONSTANT, REASSURING PRESENCE. THE MINUTE I'M ON THE WATER I FEEL LIKE I'M ON VACATION—IT ACTS LIKE A MOAT, ISOLATING US FROM OUR HECTIC LIVES.

unpretentious quality of the existing A-frame building, which suits the relaxed style of the owners and the working-class island, a place very different from the nearby Hamptons.

While this retreat is used as often as possible—usually for three-day weekends—the owner's lifestyle here is not one that he would be comfortable with on a permanent basis, preferring to be able to jump from this Robinson Crusoe existence to its complete opposite, a well-groomed one in frenetic New York. "We would love to spend a month or so on the island—the most we can ever manage is a couple of weeks—but I couldn't live there all year round. There's no culture for one thing, and when I say we're 'feral,' I don't mean that feral!"

Landscaping surrounding the house was planted at the time the house was built 11 years ago, and includes all-American swaths of lawn dotted with stands of native aspen, willow, and spruce. The house perches on the spur of a ridge, with panoramic views to federally protected Bureau of Land Management holdings. Steep gables echo the profile of the mountain range behind. Western red-cedar shingles mantling the exterior are wide and deep, so they perfectly suit the stature of the house. The rail that protects the balcony outside the guest rooms over the garage picks up the grid theme repeated in and out.

# IDAHO LODGE

The central Idaho Rockies offer superb hiking and fly-fishing—a fact that held particular appeal for a corporate executive who once worked in the state. For years, he entertained a desire to retire there. In the meantime, he decided to create a vacation retreat where he and his family could indulge their passion for outdoor recreation. Once they'd settled on a site, local architect Mark Pynn addressed their vision with a house that blends the rugged grandeur of western-style lodges with elements drawn from Craftsman and Japanese architecture. The result: A home as open and honest as all outdoors.

**ABOVE:**
Pynn constructed the massive chimneybreast from reinforced-concrete block, then veneered it with Idaho red argylite. To achieve a drystack look, mortar was placed between stones, then partially raked out from the crevices. The raised hearth is concrete, faced with honed cerulean granite.

**ABOVE LEFT:**
Checkerboard corbel accents echo grids.

**LEFT:**
Cordwood is cut to fit precisely in its hollow.

Despite their size, the great lodges commissioned by the National Parks Service for Yellowstone and Yosemite National Parks, among others, were designed to complement the landscape around them. Aware of this, the owner was eager to emulate their eco-friendly attitude in his own home. Coincidentally, architect Mark Pynn had also studied Japanese architecture, which reveres natural materials, and the Arts & Crafts movement, which extolled the honest, unfussy, handcrafted use of such materials. Correspondence zipped back and forth from Idaho to the client in the Northeast, a process so amicable that, once Pynn had drawn up his plans, only minute changes were necessary.

OPPOSITE:
The stained-pine trestle dining table measures nine feet in length—a span that allows ample elbow room for a crowd.

ABOVE LEFT:
Oak chairs, produced by the Stickley Company in New York State, are one of founder Gustav Stickley's original designs that transcend fad and fashion.

LEFT:
A game table awaits players on the stair landing on the second floor. Chandeliers, designed by Pynn, incorporate reproduction Mission-style lanterns.

RIGHT AND ABOVE:
Kitchen cabinetry is crafted of American cherry; lower cabinets replay the check motif. The backsplash and countertops are fabricated of the same material as the hearth: honed cerulean granite.

The site is modest in size, just an acre-and-a-half, and is equidistant from two of central Idaho's premier recreation areas. But it abuts a panoramic stretch of Bureau of Land Management acreage, affording spectacular views in every direction, and also providing protection from future development.

Although Pynn predicated his design on the late-nineteenth-century lodges with which the owner was familiar, he recast the concept to meet the family's twenty-first-century needs. Basically cruciform in shape, with steeply gabled roofs that converge at the

THIS PAGE:
In two guest rooms, Pynn emphasized the architectural stamina of their shared gabled roof with another gutsy play on the complex overlapping of robust structural elements; here they fan out from the corners of the ceiling into the room. The rooms are furnished sparely—but comfortably—with the bare essentials. The bed is another of Stickley's enduring designs.

center, the 5,200-square-foot house straddles a ridge, which was later landscaped with groves of willow and aspen. Just beyond the lot stretch meadows of sage, rabbit brush, wild fescue, and other native grasses. To play down the size of the house, Pynn cloaked the exterior in wide, wirebrush western red cedar shingles that have a deeper exposed surface than the norm—14 inches; these he stained a deep shade of red that softens in intensity as it weathers.

This is deep-snow country, and local building ordinances mandate a rugged roof structure to withstand the weight of accumulated snow, which can fall and drift as much as three feet in a single night. Pynn seized the opportunity to develop exterior and interior wood roof/ceiling systems based on what he terms a "hierarchy of framing members"—beams, rafters, and purlins in varying widths. In the Craftsman manner, the wood is left unpainted to dramatize what exponents of the Arts & Crafts movement would term the "honesty" of the design. The outsized proportions of the latticelike ceiling balance the grand scale of the open-plan, double-height living–dining–kitchen area.

Just as spacious upstairs as down, the house comfortably sleeps as many as 14, proving the point that the house is not only as honest as all outdoors, but just as generous in spirit, too.

## JUST BEYOND THE LOT STRETCH MEADOWS OF SAGE, RABBIT BRUSH, WILD FESCUE, AND OTHER NATIVE GRASSES.

**ABOVE LEFT:**
Arts & Crafts furniture is noted for high-quality craftsmanship and design. One of its hallmarks, seen in this side table, is the way each piece is constructed to show off its joinery, as well as the grain of the wood—usually red oak.

**ABOVE RIGHT:**
In the master bedroom, trusses spanning the window bay are accented by redwood plugs, which conceal structural-steel nuts and bolts reminiscent of traditional Japanese joinery. The armoire houses the TV.

**RIGHT:**
Recessed-panel doors, used throughout the house, illustrate yet another application of the grid theme. The recesses are shallow, so Pynn outlined them with inset square molding, to demarcate each separate square.

# PICTURE CREDITS

KEY: **a** = above, **b** = below, **c** = center, **l** = left, **r** = right, *ph* = photographer

In addition to the owners and designers mentioned above the publisher would like to thank the following:
Frank & Suz Cameron, Cathy Capri, Richard Lewis and Donna Allen, Tatjana Patitz, and Mr. & Mrs. Derald Ruttenberg.

# ARCHITECTS AND DESIGNERS

whose work has been featured in this book:

**JONATHAN ADLER**

www.jonathanadler.com

Pottery, lighting, and textiles

*Pages 6, 170br, 204–211*

**ANDERSON ARCHITECTS**

555 West 25th Street
New York
NY 10001
t. 212 620 0996
f. 212 620 5299
e. info@andersonarch.com
www.andersonarch.com

*Pages 12–13, 120ar, 121r,
146–153*

**GRETCHEN BELLINGER INC**

24 Mill Street
Albany
NY 12204
t. 518 445 2400
f. 518 445 1200
www.gretchenbellinger.com

Textile designer and owner of Camp
Bellinger

*Pages 16ar, 16br, 62–69*

**STEPHEN BLATT ARCHITECTS**

10 Danforth Street
Portland
Maine 04101
t. 207 761 5911
f. 207 761 2105
www.sbarchitects.com

Architectural design firm

*Pages 1, 18–25, 70–77*

**LAURA BOHN DESIGN
ASSOCIATES INC.**

345 Seventh Avenue, 2nd Floor
New York
NY 10001
t. 212 645 3636
f. 212 645 3639
www.lbda.com

Architecture and interior design

*Pages 50–57*

**JEFFREY CAYLE**

69 Horatio Square, Third Floor
New York
NY 10014

Designer

*Pages 130–137*

**ALEXANDRA CHAMPALIMAUD &
ASSOCIATES INC.**

One Union Square West, Suite 705
New York
NY 10003
t. 212 807 8869
f. 212 807 1742
www.alexchamp.com

Interior architecture and design

*Pages 14–15, 16al, 17b, 17ar,
34–41, 60br, 110–117*

**STEVEN CONGER ARCHITECTS**
(formerly **CONGER FULLER
ARCHITECTS**)

417 Main Street, Suite A
Carbondale
CO 81623
t: 970 963 8247
f: 970 963 8316
www.congerarchitects.com

*Pages 2–3, 60ac*

**BARBARA DAVIS**

t. 607 264 3673
www.bdavisdesigner.com

Interior design, antique hand-dyed
linens, wool and silk textiles by
yard, or soft furnishings and
clothing to order

*Pages 120al, 121al, 121bl,
154–161*

**KIRKE FORRISTAL INTERIOR
DESIGN**

18 West 9th Street
New York
NY 10011
t. 212 673 3329
f. 212 475 3371
e. suzeforristal@compuserve.com

Eclectic, comfortable, unusual
proportions with unexpected
touches

*Pages 162–167*

**MICHAEL FULLER ARCHITECTS**

t. 970 925 3021
f. 970 927 5366
www.mfullerarchitects.com

Aspen, basalt, and telluride

*Pages 2–3, 60ac*

**HOLLY LUEDERS DESIGN**

www.northstarlodgeaspen.com

Building, interior, and
furniture design

*Pages 60ar, 60bl, 78–85*

**M. J. MARCINIK
GREENMEADOW ARCHITECTS**

4046 Ben Lomond Drive
Palo Alto
California 94306
www.greenmeadow.cc

*Pages 118–119, 120br, 122–129*

**J. MORGAN PUETT**

morgan@jmorganpuett.com
www.jmorganpuett.com

*Pages 61bl, 102–109*

**MARK PYNN ARCHITECT, L.L.C.**

Post Office Box 754
Ketchum
Idaho 83340
t. 208 622 4656
f. 208 726 7108
mpynn@sunvalleyarchitect.com
www.sunvalleyarchitect.com

*Pages 4–5, 170al, 212–219*

**JIM RUSCITTO, ARCHITECT
RUSCITTO /LATHAM/BLANTON
ARCHITECTURA P.A.**

PO Box 419
Sun Valley
Idaho 83353
t. 208 726 5608
www.rib-sv.com

*Pages 61al & ar, 168–169,
172–179*

**MACK SCOGIN MERRILL ELAM
ARCHITECTS**

**Principal architects: Mack
Scogin and Merrill Elam**

111, J.W. Dobbs Avenue, N E.
Atlanta
GA 30303
t. 404 525 6869
f. 404 525 7061
www.msmearch.com

*Pages 10–11, 12a, 170bl, 170ar,
171ar, 180–187, 196–203*

**ALLAN SHOPE–ARCHITECT
SHOPE RENO WHARTON
ASSOCIATES**

18 Marshall Street, Suite 114
South Norwalk
Connecticut 06854
t. 203 852 7250
e. a.shope@srwol.com
www.shoperenowharton.com

*Pages 58–59, 94–101*

**SMITH-MILLER + HAWKINSON
ARCHITECTS LLP**

305 Canal Street
Fourth Floor
New York
NY 10013
t. 212 966 3875
f. 212 966 3877
e. contact@smharch.com
www.smharch.com

*Pages 10, 171al, 171bl, 188–195*

# Index

Numbers in *italics* refer to the captions to illustrations